Black Bibliophiles and Collectors

PRESERVERS OF BLACK HISTORY

Edited by

ELINOR DES VERNEY SINNETTE

W. PAUL COATES

THOMAS C. BATTLE

Howard University Press
Washington, D. C.
1990

Printed in the United States of America
This book is printed on acid-free paper.

Library of Congress Cataloging-in-Publication Data

Black bibliophiles and collectors : preservers of Black history /
   [edited by] Elinor Des Verney Sinnette, W. Paul Coates, Thomas C. Battle.
      p.   cm.
   Includes bibliographical references.
   ISBN 0-88258-031-0 (alk. paper) $30.00
   1. Libraries—Special collections—Afro-Americans—Congresses.
2. Afro-Americans—Library resources—Congresses. 3. Afro
Americans—Bibliography—Methodology—Congresses. 4. Afro
Americans—Manuscripts—Collectors and collecting—Congresses.
5. Afro-Americans—Historiography—Congresses. 6. Book collecting—
United States—Congresses.   I. Sinnette, Elinor Des Verney.
II. Coates, W. Paul, 1946–   . III. Battle, Thomas C.
Z688.A55B53   1990
026'.0008996073—dc20   90-4458
                                                                    CIP

Frontispiece: Bookplate of Alain LeRoy Locke, philosopher, educator, and bibliophile.
Designed by Aaron Douglass (courtesy Locke Papers, Manuscripts Department,
Moorland-Spingarn Research Center, Howard University, Washington, D.C.)

MAY   '91

CONTENTS

Contents

Contents

Contents

PART VIII
Summary and Closing Remarks

Summary

JAMES TURNER

Closing Remarks

MICHAEL R. WINSTON

Appendix A:

GALLERY OF BIBLIOPHILES

Appendix B:

BIOGRAPHIES OF CONTRIBUTORS

Index

ACKNOWLEDGMENTS

This publication is the result of the efforts of many persons, especially the participants in the "Black Bibliophiles and Collectors Symposium" that took place on November 29 and 30, 1983 at Howard University. Funds from the National Endowment for the Humanities assisted us in planning the conference and helped to ensure the publication of this volume.

We sincerely appreciate the cooperation of those participants who carefully edited their papers to be included in the book. In addition, we are grateful to those individuals and institutions that loaned materials and granted permission for excerpts from published and unpublished writings and photographs to be included in this work. Particular mention must be made of Catherine Lenix-Hooker, Assistant Chief of the Schomburg Center for Research in Black Culture, for providing immediate personal attention to our many requests.

We gratefully acknowledge the assistance of the staff of the Moorland-Spingarn Research Center, especially Marilyn Beckles, Loretta Poke, Betty Culpepper; Alex Raphael, II, and the staff of the Photoduplication Department; Roland Scott, Maricia Battle, Prints and Photographs Librarian; and Brian Jones and the staff of the Photography Department. Very special thanks are due Jean Currie Church, Manuscript Librarian, who served as the administrative assistant for the project. Her cheerful and tireless efforts kept masses of correspondence, typescripts, photographs, and memoranda organized to promote smooth transitions through each phase of the task.

Finally we must acknowledge the skilled professional guidance we received from Fay Acker and Catherine Cauman, members of the staff of the Howard University Press. We appreciate their invaluable assistance.

INTRODUCTION

For many years black bibliophiles and collectors have played a major and largely overlooked role in the collection and preservation of the documentary and cultural heritage of people of African descent. Their efforts have been particularly important because of the general failure of educational systems, libraries, research organizations, historical societies, museums, and other cultural agencies to incorporate meaningfully and accurately the black experience into the general discourse of American and world history. Although this situation has abated somewhat as a result of the increase in black awareness, a greater interest in black history, the continuing impact of the civil rights movement, and the development of black studies curricula at many educational institutions, there remains a lack of general knowledge and understanding of black history and of the significant roles played by black history collectors in the preservation of a common heritage.

These collectors have been primarily responsible for the development of major black history collections at Howard University and the New York Public Library, as well as important collections at such institutions as Fisk and Atlanta universities. Indeed, the holdings of the Library of Congress were enhanced through the efforts of Daniel Alexander Payne Murray, who worked with Librarian of Congress Herbert Putnam to develop that library's collections early in this century.

In light of the lack of knowledge about black bibliophiles and collectors, the Moorland-Spingarn Research Center (MSRC) organized a symposium to bring together scholars, students, collectors, librarians, curators, general humanists, and other interested individuals to discuss various aspects of collecting. The symposium provided an ideal opportunity to highlight and document the often unknown or frequently forgotten efforts to preserve the pan-African experience. It also served to honor Murray, Jesse E. Moorland, Arthur Alfonso Schomburg, Henry Proctor Slaughter, Richard B. Moore, C. Glen Carrington, and other preservers of the records of black achievement.

The impetus for the development of a black bibliophiles and collectors project grew out of the special interest of Dr. Elinor Sinnette and W. Paul Coates in the lives, careers, and contributions of black bibliophiles to American society and the preservation of its cultural heritage. At the time of the symposium, both Sinnette and Coates were on the staff of the MSRC's Manuscript Division. Dr. Sinnette's fascination with black bibliophiles developed over a number of years and is perhaps best exemplified by *Arthur Alfonso Schomburg: Black Bibliophile & Collector*, her impressive biography of the noted developer of the black history collections at Fisk University and at the New York Public Library. Schomburg's personal library became the basis for the special collection at what is now known as the Schomburg Center for Research in Black Culture, and Schomburg served as its curator from its establishment and during its early years of development. Paul Coates, the former owner of the Black Book bookstore, in Baltimore, Maryland, and publisher of important out-of-print works through the Black Classic Press, has long maintained a strong personal interest in collectors, particularly book collectors, because of his involvement in these two endeavors. Providentially, employment at the MSRC brought their mutual interest together and provided an atmosphere in which this interest would be nurtured and further developed.

That interest initially manifested itself in a small exhibition, "Black Bibliophiles: Preservers of Black History," which was reproduced in part as a brochure. Positive responses to this effort led Sinnette and Coates to explore other ways to broaden the general knowledge and awareness of the efforts of bibliophiles, as well as other collectors. In June 1982 they noted that there had previously been no comprehensive attempt to identify these dedicated individuals or to examine collectively the contributions of black bibliophiles and collectors as active forces in the struggle to preserve black history. To address this issue, they suggested that the MSRC develop and sponsor a national symposium to achieve the following objectives:

1. to identify and to produce a national directory of black collectors and bibliophiles;
2. to document the nature and scope of the collecting efforts of these bibliophiles and collectors;
3. to provide information about collectors and their experience in collecting;
4. to discuss the roles played by bibliophiles and collectors in preserving black history and to do so in a forum accessible to various levels of general interest and scholarly expertise;
5. to achieve a broad dissemination of information presented at the symposium through a publication of selected presentations.

Following the favorable response to the preliminary discussions of June 1982, Sinnette and Coates revised their plans, and in January 1983 they formally recommended that the MSRC undertake the project and seek funds to conduct a national symposium. The internal planning was expanded and included Sinnette and Coates; Michael R. Winston, director of the MSRC; James P. Johnson, chief librarian; and Thomas C. Battle, curator of manuscripts and acting curator of the Howard University Museum. It was determined by this planning team that it would be advisable to bring together several notable bibliophiles and collectors to assist in the planning and development of the larger project and to participate in a staff development workshop.

In March 1983 several important collectors were invited to serve as consultants and advisors to the project and to participate as a panel in a staff development workshop. This group included Dr. Dorothy Porter Wesley, the doyenne of black bibliography, who served more than forty years as curator of the Moorland-Spingarn Collection; Charles Blockson of Norristown, Pennsylvania, one of the more important current bibliophiles; Dr. Helen Armstead Johnson, developer of the Helen Armstead Johnson Foundation for Theater Research, a vast collection of materials on blacks in the theater; James Lucas of Washington, D.C., creator of the valuable Joys of Heritage collection; and Ronald Rooks of Baltimore, Maryland, a collector, appraiser, antiques dealer, and publisher of the *Black Americana Collector*. Together these individuals brought a wide range of interest, experience, and expertise to the project.

The outside advisors met with the MSRC project staff to plan the symposium. Each was very pleased that the MSRC had initiated such a project, and all were very supportive of the objectives of the symposium. The planning session resulted in the completion of the basic outline of the symposium and its components, including potential participants and the content of sessions. The successful panel discussion/workshop that followed the planning session was a lively affair attended by MSRC staff and demonstrated that the planned symposium should be able to achieve its objectives.

"Black Bibliophiles and Collectors: A National Symposium" was held at the Armour J. Blackburn University Center at Howard University on November 29 and 30, 1983, supported in part by a grant from the National Endowment for the Humanities. It consisted of a keynote address, written papers, panel discussions, an informal roundtable, and an audience participation open forum. The symposium focused on the development and state of collecting of black historical materials, the development of private and public collections, the impact of private and institutional collecting upon historical research, trends in historiography that impact upon private and institutional collecting activities, black-related memorabilia as collectibles and as material culture, and problems of security and conservation as they relate to private collections.

The symposium examined bibliopolic (buying and selling) and collecting activities of persons maintaining collections of black history and memorabilia; analyzed the roles of past and present bibliophiles and collectors in identifying, gathering, preserving, and disseminating the history and cultures of black peoples; investigated problems and advanced fresh concepts and new projects to aid further the collection and preservation of materials; identified a wide spectrum of bibliophiles and collectors in the United States, Canada, and the Caribbean; and attempted to improve communication and interaction among bibliophiles, collectors, and research repositories in an effort to advance the identification, collection, and preservation of culturally and historically valuable materials.

In this collection of selected conference papers, Dorothy Porter Wesley provides a historical perspective of black collectors and collecting through her vast knowledge of and experiences with most of the twentieth century's major bibliophiles and collectors of materials documenting black history and culture. Porter Wesley's "Black Antiquarians and Bibliophiles Revisited, with a Glance at Today's Lovers of Books and Memorabilia" is a tour de force of insight and knowledge by, perhaps, the most accomplished institutional collector of materials documenting the pan-African experience. Tony Martin's "Bibliophiles, Activists, and Race Men" concentrates on Philadelphia bibliophiles, but places their efforts within the context of racial consciousness and activism that has become an important element of identification among those who have only recently come to understand the seminal contributions of black people to world history. Robert Hill further characterizes the important relationship between black history and black activism in discussing Marcus Garvey and his unifying efforts in "On Collectors, Their Contributions to the Documentation of the Black Past." Elinor Sinnette's "Arthur Alfonso Schomburg (1874–1938), Black Bibliophile and Collector" describes the impetus that spurred one of this century's most important collectors and a developer of collections to pursue his life's work. Interested readers will be well served by acquiring and reading Sinnette's biography of this twentieth-century progenitor of black bibliography.

Since the efforts of many of the major bibliophiles and collectors are reflected in collections that form the foundations of important college, university, and public library research collections, there are several papers that describe these significant resources. Jean Blackwell Hutson discusses "The Schomburg Center for Research in Black Culture," a notable resource located in Harlem and a well-known research unit of the New York Public Library. Jessie Carney Smith describes several public collections while focusing upon the resource developed by Arthur Schomburg at Fisk University in "An Overview, Including the Special Collections at Fisk University." In "Special Collections at Atlanta University Center," Minnie Clayton discusses the important contributors to the materials that are now the foundation of special collections at the Atlanta University Center. She makes clear that the successful acquisition of pan-African history is the result of the indomitable spirit of the dedicated few for the benefit of all. The Moorland-Spingarn Research Center, celebrating seventy-five years of undaunted service to Howard University and an international community of scholars, is explored by Bettye M. Culpepper in "The Moorland-Spingarn Research Center: A Legacy of Bibliophiles."

The symposium was blessed with the presence and contributions of two of the most noted bibliophiles of recent time: Charles L. Blockson and Clarence Holte. Blockson, whose private library forms the core of a major collection at Temple University in Philadelphia, reflects upon his personal experiences in "Black Giants in Bindings." This story of the dedicated, albeit itinerant, collector should be inspirational to the novice as well as the veteran bibliophile. Holte, too, provides personal insight into collecting and expands the boundaries outside the United States. He also discusses his involvement with reprint publishing and the acquisition of his private library by Ahmadu Bello University in Zaria, Nigeria, in "The Romance of Incidental Adventures in Collecting Books."

Paul Robeson, Jr., has been responsible for pursuing one of the most significant private efforts to document the life and achievements of a single individual. His work to develop the Paul Robeson Archives and to collect the Paul and Eslanda Goode Robeson Papers is described in "The Robeson Archives." Bettye Collier-Thomas, in "Present Programs and Future Needs," identifies neglected research areas and sets an agenda for collecting primary research materials. Both Robeson and Collier-Thomas project the seriousness of purpose that is critical for all collectors attempting to reclaim the evidence essential to historical research.

One of the priorities of the symposium was to acknowledge and to support the efforts of the many private collectors who help to identify, to collect, and to preserve materials documenting the black experience. Valerie Sandoval Mwalilino offers "The Arrangement and Care of Small Book Collections." Karen Jefferson contributes "The Arrangement and Care of Manuscript Materials." Mwalilino targets the collector of books, pamphlets and monographs. Jefferson aims her remarks toward the collector of documents and the preserver of personal and organizational records.

In an event such as a symposium, it is important to establish a context. This was ably done in opening remarks by Owen D. Nichols, then vice president for administration and secretary of Howard University, and Clifford L. Muse, Jr., then acting director of the Moorland-Spingarn Research Center. Nichols noted specifically the miseducation of blacks which resulted from the omission of black contributions from much written history and textbooks, and Muse acknowledged the important roles that black bibliophiles and collectors have played in the recovery and preservation of the materials recording black achievement. Equally important are the summary and closing remarks. In his summary, James Turner reminds us of what we have omitted and encourages us to investigate further the foundations and realities of the various legacies we have inherited. We would do well to heed his advice, to build upon this effort, and to explore other avenues. Michael Winston gives us both a benediction and an invocation. While we must acknowledge and build upon past deeds, we must also identify new and effective ways to preserve and institutionalize our efforts.

"Black Bibliophiles and Collectors: A National Symposium" was not an ending. It was a beginning—an effort that must be reflected upon, absorbed, and vigorously pursued anew. These selected papers are designed to aid in that pursuit by making a wider audience more aware of the important issues discussed during the conference. We trust that the efforts of black bibliophiles and collectors will become better known and appreciated. We hope that many will be inspired by their work. The identification, collection, and preservation of information and material culture that document and reflect black history accurately are difficult and continuing endeavors. It is not enough that we simply acknowledge the efforts that have been made. We must contribute to those efforts and continue the rewarding struggle to preserve our history.

Thomas C. Battle, *Director*
Moorland-Spingarn Research Center
Howard University

PART I

Historical Perspective

BLACK ANTIQUARIANS
AND BIBLIOPHILES REVISITED,
WITH A GLANCE AT TODAY'S
LOVERS OF BOOKS AND MEMORABILIA

Dorothy Porter Wesley

Today, blacks, as a hobby or profession, collect paintings, prints, porcelains, glassware, china, dolls, Chinese objects, African art, miniatures of all kinds, and, in most recent years, black images, ugly and beautiful, usually referred to as black memorabilia. In this paper, though, I will be considering primarily collectors of books by and about blacks, books rare, unique, autographed, and association copies published during the sixteenth, seventeenth, eighteenth, nineteenth, and twentieth centuries.

All the collectors I have known have indeed been bibliophiles, since the term *bibliophile* means "lover of books." It seems to me that the two words are interchangeable. We might say bibliophiles have a passion for collecting and possessing books to such an extreme that often we refer to them as "bibliomaniacs." Once they own a book or establish a collection it is extremely difficult for them to part with their possessions. On occasion, for monetary reasons, bibliophiles have been known to sell some of their prized possessions. Several times W. E. B. Du Bois, not often thought of as a book collector, sold books, due to necessity, by black authors from his collection to the well-known collector and bibliophile Arthur Barnett Spingarn.

I feel quite certain that all librarians are lovers of books and could rightly be called bibliophiles. Bibliographers who identify and describe

Dr. Dorothy Porter Wesley is the Curator Emerita of the Moorland-Spingarn Research Center at Howard University.

MOORLAND-SPINGARN RESEARCH CENTER

THE ARTHUR B. SPINGARN COLLECTION

OF NEGRO LITERATURE

HOWARD UNIVERSITY

The bookplate of bibliophile Arthur B. Spingarn rendered by African American artist Aaron Douglass. The
Spingarn Collection, at the time of its acquisition in 1946
by Howard University, was considered the most comprehensive private collection of books written by black people. It was noted for its works by early African American
writers and its many volumes on African languages.
(Courtesy Library Division, Moorland-Spingarn
Research Center, Howard University, Washington, D.C.)

4

books are also lovers of books and, as such, are essential to the "health and well-being" of collectors and bibliophiles. The importance of librarians, archivists, and bibliographers who are also collectors and builders of our African American library collections cannot be minimized.

EARLY BEGINNINGS

It was during the first two decades of the nineteenth century that small groups of free men and women organized and developed collections of books, periodicals, and newspapers to meet the need for intellectual and moral improvement. Over 150 years ago, on March 20, 1828, a group of free men of color in Philadelphia organized a "Reading Room Society." Books were collected and a librarian appointed to see that they were loaned to members of the society for no longer than one week. *Freedom's Journal,* the first Negro newspaper, had appeared in March 1827, and it and Lundy's *Genius of Universal Emancipation,* an antislavery publication, were among the first works circulated. On January 1, 1833, the Philadelphia Library Company of Colored Persons was established and four months later in May 1833, an appeal was made for books and donations. By 1836 the Philadelphia Library Company of Colored Persons was incorporated, and in 1838 the library collection contained 600 volumes.

This activity stimulated free black people in several large cities, particularly in the East, to develop and maintain circulating libraries. Philadelphians were particularly active, and between 1828 and 1841 there were at least eight such "bookish" or literary societies in existence. Although women in Philadelphia had organized a Female Literary Society in 1831 and a Minerva Literary Association in 1834, black women did not become as avid collectors and bibliophiles as black men. The reasons for this are obvious. There were some women, however, in more recent years, such as Mary E. Moore of Boston, who developed and built a collection of black literature. Some of these books found their way to Howard University.

Probably the first black book collector was David Ruggles, an abolitionist and a printer and pamphleteer in the 1830s. He maintained a circulating library of antislavery and anti-colonization publications and made them available to many readers at a fee of less

FREEDOM'S JOURNAL.

"RIGHTEOUSNESS EXALTETH A NATION."

CORNISH & RUSSWURM,
Editors and Proprietors.

NEW-YORK, FRIDAY, JULY 13, 1827.

VOL. I.—NO. 18.

EUROPEAN COLONIES IN AMERICA.

[We recommend to the attentive perusal of our readers, the following extract from an interesting work, entitled *America, or a General Survey*, &c. &c. By a citizen of the United States.]

The republic of Hayti, without belonging precisely to the class of European colonies in America, seems to hold its independence by a somewhat doubtful tenure, (the price that is to be given for it being not yet paid,) and may be considered with propriety in the same section. Notwithstanding the very questionable character of the late transactions with France, (which does, however, quite as little honour to that powerful kingdom as to its colony,) the example of Hayti has been upon the whole of a nature to encourage the expectations of the friends of humanity, in regard to the capacity of the black race, for self-government and the arts and habits of a civilized life...

HISTORY OF SLAVERY.

As maxims which have received the sanction of several successive generations, are frequently admitted with little examination; so practices which can be traced through every period of history, are sometimes considered as the necessary result of our physical or moral organization...

(To be Continued.)

than twenty-five cents a month. Ruggles had no time to become our first bibliophile, however, because the purpose of his book collection was to enlighten as many persons as possible to the condition in which they found themselves and to improve it as quickly as possible.

A FLOWERING OF INTEREST

In less than two decades after the early Philadelphia book collections and literary societies had been founded, the city of Philadelphia became a hotbed for black collectors and scrapbook makers. The genesis of organized book collecting, particularly among black Philadelphians, and the development of black bibliophiles, such as Robert Mara Adger and William Carl Bolivar in Philadelphia, have been studied in *Rare Afro-Americana: A Reconstruction of the Adger Library*, edited by Dr. Tony Martin and Wendy Ball. James G. Spady, a Philadelphia marketing analyst, lecturer, and collector, has also presented this subject briefly in his article "The Afro-American Historical Society: The Nucleus of Black Bibliophiles, 1897–1923," in the *Negro History Bulletin* for June/July 1974. Spady illustrated his article with a handsome portrait of William Carl Bolivar, "a connoisseur in rare books." He also reproduced a photograph of Leon Gardiner, another Philadelphia collector, who did more than anyone else to salvage the remains of the early black collections, including books and papers accumulated by the Philadelphia historical societies and the black bibliophiles of Philadelphia.

Another significant work in this area is Betty Kaplan Gubert's *Early Black Bibliographies, 1863–1918*, in which the catalogue of the library of William Carl Bolivar was reproduced, as well as a list of books collected by Robert Mara Adger, including his rare books and pamphlets, priced and ready for sale. Since both Adger and Bolivar

---

Facing page: Freedom's Journal was the first newspaper published in the United States by African Americans. Founded by John Russwurm and Samuel Cornish and first published on March 16, 1827, it clearly stated its intent: "We wish to plead our own cause." Although short-lived, *Freedom's Journal* had a lasting impact. (Courtesy Library Division, Moorland-Spingarn Research Center, Howard University, Washington, D.C.)

disposed of their collections, it is a pity they kept no narrative reports about when, where, and how they acquired their books, and especially the prices they paid for them. It would also have enhanced the value of their once personal books if these bibliophiles had a bookplate designed by an artist, placed in all their books, never to be removed by librarians or others who might finally acquire them. A bookplate was made by artist James A. Porter and placed in most of the books belonging to Frederick Douglass many years after he died, but only a few black collectors have identified their treasures with bookplates. Philadelphia produced other black collectors. Isaiah Wears, William Henry Dorsey, Leon Gardiner, and Joseph W. H. Cathcart were all contemporaries of Adger and Bolivar.

Joseph W. H. Cathcart, a janitor of a building located at 303 Walnut Street in Philadelphia, although not a learned man, was a great reader of newspapers. His desire to preserve the good things and some bad things he read about black people in newspapers forced him in 1856 to begin making scrapbooks of newspaper clippings. By 1882, he had compiled 100 huge volumes. Cathcart's neatly bound scrapbooks covered a variety of happenings over a quarter of a century. Each volume of four inches or more in width had the subject stamped in gold on the back, with the name of the compiler followed by the mysterious letters "G.S.B.M.," meaning "Great Scrap-Book Maker." The first clipping in Cathcart's first book was dated December 16, 1856, and was an advertisement offering a reward for the capture of a runaway slave. The last volume contained a pamphlet entitled "Mayor King and His Black Policemen" and was made up of newspaper articles relating to the appointment of black men to the Philadelphia Police force.

John Wesley Cromwell, a Washington book lover and close associate of the Philadelphia, New York, and Boston collectors, was one of the founders and secretary of the American Negro Academy. Cromwell was associated with collectors Henry Proctor Slaughter, Arthur A. Schomburg, and Alain LeRoy Locke. Cromwell acquired the Cathcart scrapbooks probably through purchase. In 1900, they found their way into the Carnegie Library at Howard University and were spoken of as "The Cromwell Collection." When I was put in charge of the Negro collection I found many of these large black volumes in the stacks adjacent to my reading room on the second floor of the old

Carnegie Library, which housed the Negro Collection and which was next to the office of President Mordecai Johnson.

The volumes most valuable for research purposes were entitled "The Colored People and the Passenger Railroads," "The Fifteenth Amendment," two or three volumes entitled "The Black Man After the Passage of the Civil Rights Bill," and "John Brown's Insurrection"—a volume Dr. Benjamin Quarles found very helpful for his book on John Brown and the Negro, *Allies for Freedom: Blacks and John Brown*—and several volumes on "The Freedmen's Bureau." Many other titles of Cathcart's scrapbooks are listed in a newspaper article in the *Times* (of Philadelphia), dated February 27, 1882, and in *The Sunday Dispatch*, dated March 20, 1881. *The Peoples Advocate*, October 6, 1877, also carried an article on these scrapbooks. It was fifty years ago that I first saw these volumes in the Carnegie Library of Howard University.

One day during the first year of my assignment to build a Negro collection, a member of the Cromwell family entered the reading room unannounced and stated that the scrapbooks did not belong to Howard University, that they were on loan and were now to be returned to the Cromwell home. At the time I could find no record indicating that the scrapbooks had been purchased by or given to the university. Thus, the large volumes containing a storehouse of information were removed from our shelves, placed in a truck, and driven to 1814 13th Street, N. W., the Cromwell family home at that time.

The story about the coming and going and returning of the Cathcart Collection is an involved one. It seems that a member of the Cromwell family, John W. Cromwell, Jr., an employee of Howard University, had lost his job. He had been a classmate of my father's at the university. My mother had often played bridge with him and friends on her visits to D.C. I, too, had had a relationship with a Cromwell family member, Dr. Otelia Cromwell, for whom I was able to borrow a number of manuscripts from a California library for use in a book she was writing. Since she was the person who came for the scrapbooks, it may very well have been that she wanted to use them for her own research. I talked, however, to my good spirits and eventually one cold night with ice on the ground, I was able to retrieve the scrapbooks from an area next to the oil heater in the basement of the Cromwell's 13th Street home and bring most of them back to the university. I had made a list of the volumes, and they all did not come back. During all the years that the volumes were used by scholars, it was not until 1976 after I had retired that I learned who Cathcart was or who had compiled those valuable books.

A close friend of Cathcart was William Henry Dorsey, the son of a well-known Philadelphia caterer, who also compiled valuable scrapbooks on many subjects. Approximately 410 of them found their way into the archives of Cheyney State College. Dorsey, an artist and bibliophile, maintained for many years a museum in the front room of the second story of his home. In addition to books, prints, engravings, and manuscripts, he collected coins, minerals, implements of warfare used by "barbarous nations," oil and water color paintings by well-known artists, such as Robert Duncanson, music by African American composers, steel and copper engravings, and photographs of prominent blacks.

Philadelphia was not the only city where black collectors and bibliophiles thrived. In Boston, New York City, Washington, D.C., and Cincinnati, large circles of bibliophiles were formed. They exchanged books, corresponded with each other, and visited one another regularly. Each competed with the other in a friendly way in an attempt to acquire the largest number and rarest volume of books by black authors.

Interest in collecting books by black authors became so widespread that a number of men meeting at dinner at the home of John Wesley Cromwell, Sr., organized the Negro Book Collectors Exchange in 1915, during a session of the American Negro Academy. The purpose of the Book Collectors Exchange was to centralize all literature written by colored persons. The Exchange was to "contact all Negro Book Collectors throughout the United States, Africa, the West Indies, South America and Europe" and request copies of books written by Negro authors. A bibliography of all black authors and their works was planned. The officers were all serious bibliophiles. Henry Proctor Slaughter, the Washington collector, was named president, and John Cromwell was chosen vice president. The New Yorker Arthur Alfonso Schomburg was elected secretary-treasurer and his fellow New York collector, the Reverend Charles Douglass Martin, was named librarian. John Edward Bruce, another New York bibliophile, served as publicity agent and Daniel Alexander Murray of Washington, D.C. was named registrar. I have my personal reminiscences of these men—particularly

COLORED COLLECTORS

Negro Antiquarians Interested in Historical Research.

THE DORSEY COLLECTION

Efforts of Robert Adger, Jr., to Assemble Memorials of the Slavery Struggle.

It would seem that the colored people were too poor to become collectors in one sense of the word, and yet if a lover of antiques, a lover of historical books, pamphlets and pictures were to go among them he would possibly be surprised. The Dorsey collection is well known as a collection of race literature and souvenirs. Begun in the lifetime of the older Thomas Dorsey, it has been constantly enriched by the son until it contains many historical works, coins and other antiques.

The interest the negro is taking in himself is shown all over the country, and especially in Philadelphia, by this tendency to collect all facts of interest to the race, or which show the progress they are making toward overcoming prejudice. A very interesting collection is that of Robert Adger, Jr. Mr. Adger was given employment in the Post Office under General Huidekoper, and has remained there until the present date. During this time he has made many friends who have become interested in his collection of pictures of the friends and foes of freedom, and have given him kindly assistance in carrying out his plan, many gentlemen having placed their autographs under the picture sent them when they were told of the intention of the collector.

Granville Sharp, the pioneer of emancipation in the West Indies; Judges Taney, Scott and Nelson, Judges Curtis and McClean, opposing counsel in the Dred Scott case; Dred Scott and wife, Elijah Lovejoy, who was the first martyr to the cause of emancipation, being murdered at Alton, Ill., November 7, 1837, all have places in the collection as well as Prudence Crandall, who was mobbed for opening a school for colored girls in Massachusetts and who was given a contribution in her old age, raised through Mr. Fortune, of the New York *Age*; Douglass, Langston, Whipper, Purvis and the martyred Catto, friends and members of the race; A. M. Powell, editor of the *Anti-Slavery Standard*; Joshua R. Giddings and Ashman, presiding officers of the convention that nominated Abraham Lincoln for the Presidency; Wendell Phillips, William Lloyd Garrison, Lincoln and John Brown, Charles Sumner and Preston Brocks, his assailant, and Anson V. Burlingame, who espoused the cause of Sumner. In addition, are to be seen the leaders of the secession, the opposing generals of the civil war, James L. Pettigrew, the only Union man in Charleston, S. C., at the time of the breaking out of the rebellion; Stephen Smith and wife, who contributed largely to the opening of the Old Folks' Home of Philadelphia, and numbers of groups of authors, artists and statesmen. The collection is not only unique from the point stated, but the frames are made entirely of waste paper from the cancelling department of the Post Office. These clippings imitate oak and maple frames and are durable and beautiful. On the back, after placing the glass in position, is placed another paper covering and on the back of this the newspaper clipping giving important facts. A tiny brass ring and ribbon completes the frame, the whole collection being placed in a tiny room, neatly hung and worthy of careful survey.

M. Adger acted as usher at Independence Square during the one hundredth anniversary of the Constitution of the United States. He was presented by Hampton L. Carson with a copy of the two historical volumes that commemorate that occasion. Judge J. T. Miller wrote his autograph under the picture of himself in this work. Mr. Adger has valuable files of old newspapers, and some unique bric-a-brac are also to be found in the collection.

An oil painting of Anthony Benezet, the member of the Society of Friends who opened the first school for colored children in Philadelphia, is in the possession of Mrs. N. F. Mossell. Several well-known colored people of literary tastes have made interesting and valuable collections of the writings of the race and of all literature bearing on the negro problem. The poems of Phyllis Wheatley, over 100 years old, published in London, the "Higher Grade Colored Society of Philadelphia," "An Enquiry Concerning the Intellectual and Moral Faculties and Literature of Negroes," published in Paris by the Bishop of Blois and in 1810 translated by D. B. Warden, secretary to the American Legation at Paris; "The Tribute of the Negro" and all the later works by black and white authors, such as Fortune, George Williams, Cable, Tourgee and others, are being carefully gathered. In the keeping of Horace J. Smith, a philanthropist, a member of the Society of Friends and an earnest friend of the negro, is an interesting document preserved since 1688. Mr. Smith's ancestors were among the original settlers of Pennsylvania, and by this means he has fallen heir to this precious document, the original protest against slavery drawn up over two hundred years ago by Francis Daniel Pastorius. Much matter of interest relating to the history of the negro in this country and State is in the possession of the Society of Friends and the colored people. The colored people are not wealthy enough to support a historical society of their own, but have long been discussing some method of preserving the facts and valuables on this subject where they will be safe and easy of access to the race and those interested in their welfare.

"Colored Collectors," *Times* (of Philadelphia), February 8, 1890. This article mentions the collection and collecting efforts of Thomas and William Dorsey of Philadelphia, Pennsylvania and describes the important efforts of Robert Adger, Jr., to document and preserve black history. (Courtesy Dorsey Collection, Manuscripts Department, Moorland-Spingarn Research Center, Howard University, Washington, D.C.)

of my friend Henry Proctor Slaughter, whose library occupied three floors and a basement in his town house at 1264 Columbia Road, N.W., Washington, D.C.

Slaughter acquired many of the books in his collection from his friend "Billy Bolivar." While his rare books occupied the tops of dressers and small bookcases in all his bedrooms, his book stacks, specially built on the top floor, held in classified arrangement his slavery and Civil War books. Henry Slaughter purchased many of his books from English booksellers, tucking in each the sales slips.

His collection of books in very fine bindings was unique and he presented one to me as a birthday gift. At another time, I received from him as a gift a 1773 first edition of Phillis Wheatley poems. Charles Blockson, the avid Pennsylvania collector, may not know that the book which I gave him several years ago, *Sketches of Higher Classes of Colored Society in Philadelphia*, published anonymously in 1841 and identified as the work of Joseph Wilson, had been given to me by Henry Slaughter. Since I do not call myself a collector, I sometimes like to present rare or special volumes to young collectors who have followed in the tradition of our antiquarian bibliophiles. There are many dozens of unmentioned antiquarian book collectors I have admired and loved. They have been most certainly preservers of our black history.

BLACK BIBLIOPHILES AT HOWARD UNIVERSITY

There have been many black bibliophiles who were also some of the great teachers at Howard University and who helped build our Moorland-Spingarn Research Center—Benjamin Brawley, for example, who, in addition to his collection of books on black literature and social history, acquired one of the largest, if not one of the most complete, collections of works, printed and in manuscript, by and about Richard Le Gallienne. It consisted of first and limited editions, many of which were autographed. Brawley bequeathed this unique collection and his collection of books by and about black authors to Howard University. Charlotte Schuster Price, a former manuscript librarian in the Moorland-Spingarn Collection, compiled an annotated bibliography of the Le Gallienne Collection and a descriptive list of the manuscripts with an introduction. This study was published by Howard University Libraries in 1973, in its Occasional Papers Series, "Consciousness IV Project," during the directorship of William D. Cunningham.

While Charles Eaton Burch, professor of English and head of the Department of English from 1933 until his death on March 23, 1948, did not collect books written by black writers, he did, in the early 1920s, introduce a course "Poetry and Prose of Negro Life," one of the first devoted to black literature in an American university. Burch, a specialist in the area of eighteenth-century English literature, was an authority on the life and works of Daniel Defoe. He assembled a remarkable collection of works by and about Defoe that Velma McLin Mitchell, a Howard University graduate student, compiled into a catalogue. For some time I had seen the old antique-appearing books quietly reposing on library shelves. Then in 1973 when I had planned to write a paper on Charles Eaton Burch as a collector, for the Charles Burch memorial lecture that I was to give on March 30, I learned that the books had disappeared. After fruitless attempts, I have had to give up the search for them. His papers and correspondence, however, were saved and added to the Moorland Collection. I will always remember Dr. Burch's rosy complexion, broad smile, and his energetic walk as he entered the Moorland Reading Room to show me a recent Defoe acquisition, or when he brought a donation for the library—Daniel Payne's *Diary* for example, and other works pertaining to our interest.

A lengthy essay should be written about the collecting idiosyncrasies of Alain LeRoy Locke. I knew Locke well as my teacher of philosophy and as a colleague. It took me days and days to unpack several collections of books, manuscripts, artifacts, phono-recordings, and oddities he bequeathed to the Moorland Collection. The university art gallery received his extensive African art collection. Locke was indeed a collector, perhaps not a bibliophile. It is unbelievable what this critic, philosopher, and leader did collect—and collect he did! He saved his books, every scrap of paper, thousands of manuscripts, photographs, medical x-rays, ticket stubs, train schedules, gas bills, and countless notes taken from almost any book or periodical to suit his research purposes. Locke even kept fragile, deteriorated Christmas toys from his boyhood days. One object is a large piece of old wood sent to Locke by Zora Neale Hurston, who claimed it was from the helm of the last slave ship that arrived in Florida where she lived. Locke had become a Bahai before his death and his collection of books on that faith has been of interest to other local Bahais. When future biographers of Locke reconstruct his collecting activities, much about the man will be revealed.

The anniversary of the eightieth birthday of Dr. Mark Hanna Watkins was November 23, 1983. A brilliant anthropologist, sociologist and linguist, he was a professor of anthropology at Howard University from 1947 until his death in February 1976. As a specialist in South African Bantu languages, the Creole dialects of Haiti, the

Alain LeRoy Locke (1885–1954), philosopher, critic, and educator, was the first African American Rhodes Scholar. Locke was born in Philadelphia, Pennsylvania and spent most of his career on the faculty of Howard University. He was an early proponent at Howard of study and research on race, colonialism, and culture. Locke is best known for his early promotion of the New Negro movement, which is commonly known today as the Harlem Renaissance. (Courtesy Locke Papers, Manuscripts Department, Moorland-Spingarn Research Center, Howard University, Washington, D.C.)

Cakchiquel language in Guatemala, and the Cabeka language in Costa Rica, Dr. Watkins built an extensive collection of dictionaries, language books, sociological and anthropological treatises, and specialized periodicals. His doctoral dissertation, published in 1937 by the Linguistic Society of America and entitled "A Grammar of Chichewa, A Bantu Language of British Central Africa," has been regarded as a pioneering and fundamental study in African linguistics. As an aid to his studies, Dr. Watkins acquired a unique and rare book and periodical collection in linguistics and anthropology.

Other Howard University professors and members of the Board of Trustees who had substantial collections of books and materials relating to their special fields were Walter G. Dyson, Carter G. Woodson, Charles H. Wesley, Rayford W. Logan, A. Mercer Daniel, Montgomery Gregory, Owen Dodson, W. Montague Cobb, and Frances J. Grimke.

COLLECTORS AND THEIR CATALOGS

As a bibliographer, I had always wished that our antiquarian and other collectors would have compiled for us checklists of their collections with brief annotations or notes. The catalogs of Robert Adger's collection were sale catalogs. Daniel Murray's list was prepared for the American Negro Exhibit at the Paris Exhibition of 1900, while Bolivar's friends presented him with a printed list of his collection as a birthday surprise in May 1914.

The published eulogy, delivered by Henry L. Phillips at Bolivar's funeral services, included a photograph of Bolivar reading a book while sitting in an armchair. I have in my print collection a larger version of this same photograph, which more clearly shows a large number of framed pictures of babies and adults, extended bookshelves, a woman's shoe kicked off her foot, and Bolivar wearing very worn laced shoes with cigar in hand, reading a book. Bolivar had to read. How else could he store in his memory the many facts used in the obituaries and articles on Philadelphia history that he contributed for twenty-two years, under the pen name of "Pencil Pusher," to the *Philadelphia Tribune?*

A Treasure Trove, A Bibliography of a Collection of African and Afro-American Books was issued anonymously in 1965 in New York City, with the intent of selling about 125 items in the possession of one of the greatest living collectors of Africana and Afro-Americana, Clarence L. Holte, the New York City collector. I was fortunate enough to visit Holte's apartment and the additional apartment he had acquired in the building for his ever-expanding collection. I also followed his trail in Nigeria, especially to Abeokuta, where he was collecting ephemera, pamphlets, and Nigerian books in the vernacular for Nnamdi Azikiwe, former president of Nigeria, himself a great collector before the Biafran war. The largest part of Clarence L. Holte's collection was purchased by Ahmadu Bello University in Zaria, Nigeria. Charlayne Hunter-Gault described Holte's 7,000 books on black literature and history in the *New York Times* on March 18, 1972.

BOOK COLLECTING TODAY

In this decade, there are many young and not so young black professionals who are book collectors of rare African and Afro-American books and art works, in spite of the fact that the quantity of rarities has diminished in the last twenty years. When they are available, the asking price is exorbitant.

I searched for fifty years for a copy of the first edition of *The House Servant's Directory* by Robert Roberts, a black abolitionist, which I finally purchased from bookseller William Reese. This interesting book was first published in 1827, and not in 1828 as described in volume two, number three, of *The Schomburg Center Journal*. In fact, there were three editions and the book has been reprinted recently. In 1933, I was able to locate only six copies in libraries.

Today we are learning about men and women from the East Coast to the West who have substantial collections of black memorabilia that seem to fall into two categories: "derogatory collectibles and artifacts" and items of "beauty and dignity."

In January 1980, I visited The Du Sable Museum in Chicago and saw there an exhibition of a small part of The Victor Travis Collection of Stereotypes of African and Afro-Americans. The collection designated as "Popular Culture" was organized into the following categories: Realtypes, the surrogate parents (robust mammies and kindly ole "uncles"); watermelon eaters; jungle bunnies; exploitation photographs; products and packaging; cartoons; and the children's corner. Mr. Travis, a special education teacher in the Chicago public schools, lives with his wife in Gary, Indiana.

Harriet Stiks's *Black Images in the White Mind* describes the collection of black images of Janette Faulkner, a psychiatric social worker in California. Her collection, one of the most comprehensive of its kind, includes items dating back to 1847. Miss Faulkner, who calls her exhibition "Ethnic Notions: Black Images in the White Mind," has included lawn ornaments, toys, milk jugs, baby plates, post cards, advertisements. The collection also includes sheet music and numerous objects, for example, the Topsy Turvy dolls with a black face at one end and which, with a flip of the skirt, show a white face at the other end.

Paula Parker's *Contemptible Collectibles* tells us that Mary Kimbrough, a dental hygienist in Los Angeles, has 1,400 pieces of black memorabilia that portray black Americans as "subhuman symbols of racism in its concretest form." Included are commodities that helped blacks survive slavery, such as cotton, watermelons, and chickens, and numerous other objects like mammies, cooks, butlers, and porters, which depict African Americans as servants, cooks, and cleaning women. Mrs. Kimbrough's collection consists of items made in the United States, Germany, Great Britain, and Japan. A graduate of Howard University, Mrs. Kimbrough has stated that she knows at least a dozen people who collect "hate memorabilia" not only of blacks, but other minorities.

John Harris, before his death, collected eighteenth- and nineteenth-century American and British tokens, antislavery medals, and badges. His collection numbered approximately 500. In 1979, he received the Numismatic Ambassador Award, a prestigious honor conferred by Krause Publications, a leading numismatic publishing firm.

In a small house on a quiet street in Hagerstown, Maryland, Marguerite Doleman is preserving the history of Washington County's black community. Growing rapidly during the last ten years, Mrs. Doleman's doll collection, pot-bellied stove, handsome quilts, copies of Bible records from black families, bills of sale for slaves, stamps commemorating blacks, and other items give evidence of the life and contributions of blacks in Washington County. She has recently published a pamphlet entitled *We the Blacks of Washington County.*

Local collectors of black memorabilia include Naomi Wright, who collects black American objects of beauty made around the world along with rare glassware; Kathleen Snowden of Maryland, who collects anything relating to black history, especially documents, many of which she has found in old trunks; and Dr. Lillian Anthony, who has collected 2,500 derogatory images of blacks. She began her collection twenty years ago when she was researching the topic "Why Black Women are Portrayed Negatively on Television and in Books."

Her items date from the mid-1850s to the present. Ronald Rooks, a Baltimore antiques dealer and collector, specializes in documents, prints, photos, and letters. There are other collectors of black historical materials in the Washington area, Carlton Funn and William Layton among them.

The *Washington Post*, on May 5, 1983, published a picture and story about James "Money Man" McClain, who has turned his home at 726 3rd Street, N. E., into a museum. Since 1967, he has been collecting photographs, posters, and memorabilia. A sign over the front of his house reads "Money Man's Capitol Hill Home Sweet Home." Beneath the sign there are posters, carousel horses, and "junk"—plenty of it. Each room inside the house has a name— Museum Guest Room, The Chapel Room, Jukebox and Picture Museum Room, Sexy Bathrooms, and Money Man's Sex Room—his bedroom. Thus we see there are all kinds of collectors.

Finally, among black collectors today there is Dr. Marguerite Ross, a professor of political science at Columbia University, who has been collecting black memorabilia for many years. She has just published a book, *Images of Blacks in American Popular Culture, 1865–1955*.

Is this new collecting field of black images booming because of the scarcity of rare research books and pamphlets—the materials that attracted our antiquarian book collectors of yesteryear? This volume, *Black Bibliophiles and Collectors*, will answer that question. This book will also attest to the fact that there are collectors and bibliophiles of African and African American materials who are continuing in the tradition of the antiquarians. They will one day become antiquarians themselves and prepare another generation of collectors and biblio- philes to take their place.

SOURCES

Atlanta University, Trevor Arnett Library. *Guide to Manuscripts and Archives in the Negro Collection of Trevor Arnett Library, Atlanta University*. Atlanta: Trevor Arnett Library, 1971, 13–17.

Ball, Wendy, and Tony Martin. *Rare Afro-Americana: A Reconstruction of the Adger Library*. Boston: G. K. Hall, 1981.

"Death of William C. Bolivar." *Christian Recorder*, Nov. 19, 1914.

"The Great Scrap-Book Maker" [J. W. H. Cathcart]. *The Times* (Philadelphia), Feb. 27, 1882.

Gubert, Betty Kaplan. *Early Black Bibliographies, 1863–1918.* New York and London: Garland, 1982.

Gumby, L. S. A. "The Gumby Scrapbook Collection of Negroana." *Columbia Library World* 5, no. 1 (1951).

Harris, Jr., R. L. "Daniel Murray and *The Encyclopedia of the Colored Race.*" *Phylon* (Sept. 1976): 270–82.

———. "Daniel Alexander Payne Murray." In *Dictionary of American Negro Biography,* edited by Rayford W. Logan and Michael R. Winston, 463–65. New York: W. W. Norton, 1982.

Hunter, Charlayne. "7,000 Books on Blacks Fill a Home." *The New York Times,* March 18, 1972.

Kaiser, E. "John Edward Bruce." In *Dictionary of American Negro Biography,* edited by Rayford W. Logan and Michael R. Winston, 76–77. New York: W. W. Norton, 1982.

Lee, E. A. "Daniel Murray," *The Colored American Magazine* 5, no. 6 (October 1902): 432–40.

MacPherson, Myra. "Uncolored Black History." *The Washington Post,* July 31, 1972. Concerning Carlton Funn's Collection of African Heritage—The Afro-American Experience and other Minorities. See also article in *Afro-American Newspaper,* March 10, 1970.

Mitchell, V. E. McL. "Charles Eaton Burch: A Scholar and His Library." *College Language Association Journal* 16, no. 3 (1973): 369–76. Dr. Burch, a Howard University professor and bibliophile, collected rare and unusual books by and about Daniel Defoe and works by eighteenth-century men of letters.

Murray, D. "Bibliographer of Afro-American Literature in the Library of Congress." *The Colored American Magazine* 5, no. 6 (October 1902): 432–40.

———. comp. *Preliminary List of Books and Pamphlets by Negro Authors for Paris Exhibition and Library of Congress.* Compiled for the American Negro Exhibit, Paris Exhibition of 1900, Thos. J. Calloway, Special Agent, 8 pages.

———. "Bibliographia Africania." *The Voice of the Negro* 1 (May 1904): 186–91.

Phillips, Henry L. A Eulogy Delivered by Henry L. Phillips in St. Thomas P. E. Church, Philadelphia, Pa., November 16, 1914, at the burial service of the late William Carl Bolivar. n.d., 10 pages.

Porter, D. B. "Bibliography and Research in Afro-American Familiar and Less Familiar Sources." *African Studies Bulletin* 12, no. 3 (Dec. 1969): 293–303.

———. "Family Records, a Major Resource for Documenting the Black Experience in New England." Old-Time New England. *The Bulletin of the Society for the Preservation of New England Antiquities* 68, no. 3 (Winter 1973): 69–72.

———. "Fifty Years of Collecting." Introduction to *Black Access: A Bibliography of Afro-American Bibliographies,* compiled by Richard Newman, Westport, Conn: Greenwood Press, 1984.

———. "Henry Proctor Slaughter." In *Dictionary of American Negro Biography,* edited by Rayford W. Logan and Michael R. Winston, 558–59. New York: W. W. Norton, 1982.

———. "Library Sources for the Study of Negro Life and History." *The Journal of Negro Education* 5, no. 2 (April 1936): 232–44.

———. "The Organized Educational Activities of Negro Literary Societies, 1828–1846." *The Journal of Negro Education* 5 (Oct. 1936): 556–76.

Price, Charlotte S. *Richard Le Gallienne as Collector by Benjamin Griffith Brawley: An*

Annotated Bibliography and Descriptive List of Manuscripts. Washington, D.C.: Howard University Libraries, 1973. 32 pages. (Consciousness IV, Occasional Papers Series, 1/1/73)

Redding, Saunders. "Benjamin Griffith Brawley." In *Dictionary of American Negro Biography*, edited by Rayford W. Logan and Michael R. Winston, 60–61. New York: W. W. Norton, 1982.

"A Remarkable Literary Curiosity" [Scrapbook Collection of J. H. W. Cathcart]. *Sunday Dispatch* (Philadelphia), March 20, 1881.

"A Rare Collection" [Scrapbook Collection of J. H. W. Cathcart]. *People's Advocate*, October 6, 1877.

Schomburg, Arthur A. *First Annual Exhibition of Books, Manuscripts, Paintings, Engravings, Sculptures*, et cetera. [Exhibition Catalogue].

"By The Negro Library Association at the Carlton Avenue Young Men's Christian Association, 405 Carlton Avenue Brooklyn, August 7 to 16 1918." Compiled by Arthur A. Schomburg, director of the Research Section, and Robert T. Browne, president. Price 25 cents. n., 3–23.

Sinnette, Elinor Des Verney. *Arthur Alfonso Schomburg, Black Bibliophile and Collector, A Biography.* Detroit: Wayne State University Press, 1989.

Spady, James G. "The Afro-American Historical Society: The Nucleus of Black Bibliophiles, 1897–1923." *Negro History Bulletin* (June/July 1974): 254–57.

———. "Leon Gardiner." In *Dictionary of American Negro Biography*, edited by Rayford W. Logan and Michael R. Winston, 251–52. New York: W. W. Norton, 1982.

———. "Robert Mara Adger." In *Dictionary of American Negro Biography*, edited by Rayford W. Logan and Michael R. Winston, 6–7. New York: W. W. Norton, 1982.

———. "William Carl Bolivar." In *Dictionary of American Negro Biography*, edited by Rayford W. Logan and Michael R. Winston, 50. New York: W. W. Norton, 1982.

Stiks, Harriet. "Black Images in the White Mind," *Americana*, vol. 10 (March–April, 1982), 22.

Treasure Trove Book Service. P.O. Box 3503, Grand Central Station, New York, N.Y. 10017. African and Afro-American books for sale by Clarence L. Holte.

Trescott, Jacqueline. "The Long, Full Life of Montague Cobb; D.C.'s Leonardo: Doctor, Teacher, Historian, Activist." *Washington Post*, November 3, 1982. Cobb is a collector of black medical history. See "The Black American in Medicine." *Journal of the National Medical Association* 73, Supplement (December 1981).

Watkins, C. C. "Charles Eaton Burch." In *Dictionary of American Negro Biography*, edited by Rayford W. Logan and Michael R. Winston, 77–79. New York: W. W. Norton, 1982.

Wayman, H. Harrison. "The American Negro Historical Society of Philadelphia Offices." *The Colored American Magazine* 6 (February 1903): 287–94. Contains sketches and pictures of Adger, Dorsey, and others.

Winston, M. R. "Alain LeRoy Locke." In *Dictionary of American Negro Biography*, edited by Rayford W. Logan and Michael R. Winston, 398–404. New York: W. W. Norton, 1982.

PART II

The Development of Early Private Collections

BIBLIOPHILES, ACTIVISTS,

AND RACE MEN

Tony Martin

There is much in the history of Africans in North America of which we can be very proud. Sometimes it has happened in our periods of despair and frustration that we have tended to emphasize negative facets of our history. Sometimes we have complained that black people will not follow black leadership. There may be some truth to this but then we study our history and we see the examples of people like Elijah Mohammed, Malcolm X, and so many others, and we know that this proposition is not entirely true.

Sometimes we have complained that black people will not financially support black organizations. Again, there may be some truth to this, but when we peruse our history we come upon a figure like Marcus Garvey, who mobilized unprecedented financial resources from the nickels and dimes of black people and we know that this complaint is not necessarily always true.

There have been complaints that we do not take our education seriously and yet if we look at the history of our people in the years during and after Reconstruction we see here one of the great epics in the history of any people: that drive to make literate those who in 1865 were 95 percent illiterate. So we know that this complaint, too, is not necessarily 100 percent true. We complain on occasion that our intellectuals have deserted their community from time to time in their attempt to win white acceptance. Here, too, there may be some truth to this allegation, but when we look at the black bibliophiles we see that this proposition is not necessarily true.

Tony Martin is professor and chairman of black studies at Wellesley College, Massachusetts.

The black bibliophiles of Afro-America, and particularly those of Philadelphia on whom I will concentrate, embody many of the positive aspects of our history in North America. They exemplify the ability of black people to follow black leadership. They exemplify the ability of our intellectuals to be socially responsible and to work for the benefit not only of themselves but for the rehabilitation of our past and for the hope of future generations. Black bibliophiles are the unsung. We need to sing their praises.

Black bibliophiles run through our history like an unseen hand. Their influence is present in many of the major developments of our historical experience, even when a superficial glance does not immediately bring to light their presence. They were the ones who built our first libraries. They were behind our first literary and debating societies. They were the ones who established our first historical societies. They were the unseen influence even in some of our mass political organizations, such as the Universal Negro Improvement Association. They left us a legacy without which the movement toward black studies in the 1960s and 1970s would have been a much more difficult effort. All of these propositions can be illustrated by reference to the black bibliophiles of Philadelphia in the nineteenth and early twentieth centuries.

BLACK BIBLIOPHILES OF PHILADELPHIA

Who were these black bibliophiles of Philadelphia? In an age when the vast majority of the black population was enslaved and/or illiterate, these people represented a nucleus of literate African Americans. By any objective standard one could call them middle class. In fact, many of them were exceedingly wealthy by anybody's standards, even by contemporary standards. One or two were even reputed millionaires. Some were merchants, like William Still of the Underground Railroad fame, who was a coal merchant in Philadelphia. Some were post office workers, like Robert Mara Adger, who was also a furniture merchant at some time in his life. Some were teachers and journalists, like William Carl Bolivar, who wrote for a couple of decades in the *Philadelphia Tribune* and who taught history in Philadelphia. Some were preachers, like the Reverend Henry L. Phillips of the Church of the Crucifixion, a Protestant Episcopal church at Eighth and

Bambridge streets in Philadelphia. Some were caterers, lawyers, and physicians such as the three generations of Mintons: Henry Minton the caterer; Theophilus J. Minton, his son, a lawyer; and Dr. Henry M. Minton, a physician and founder and superintendent of a hospital.

These people, apart from pursuing their respective occupations, were also book collectors in a variety of modes. Some bought private collections. All of them helped to build organizational collections in addition to their private collections. Robert Mara Adger, who lived from 1837 to 1910, is among those who built private collections. Adger was a book seller as well as a book collector. He was, throughout his life, involved in just about every single movement for racial uplift that was in Philadelphia, whether sporting clubs or black political organizations such as the Republican party. In 1854 at the age of seventeen, he joined one of the pioneer African American literary and debating societies, the Banneker Literary Institute. By the time he was in his mid-twenties, he was the president of the Banneker Literary Institute. His father before him was an abolitionist who was interested both in books and in uplifting the race.

In 1894 Robert Adger produced his first catalog which he entitled *A Portion of a Catalog of Rare Books and Pamphlets Collected by R.M. Adger, Philadelphia - upon Subjects Relating to the Past Condition of the Colored Race and the Slavery Agitation in this Country.* This catalog contained sixty-five titles of books, prints, and other types of artifacts that usually grace the catalogs of bibliophiles. In 1906, Adger published a second catalog upon which our knowledge of him is largely based. It bore the title *Catalog of Rare Books on Slavery and Negro Authors on Science, History, Poetry, Religion, Biography, etc. From the Private Collection of Robert M. Adger.*

This 1906 collection of Adger's found its way by a very devious route to Wellesley College. In 1906 Robert Adger sold his books to Ella Smith Albert in Wilmington, Delaware. Ms. Albert was the second black student to graduate from Wellesley College. She had graduated with a B.A. in 1888 and she remained a very active alumna of Wellesley College. In 1938 at the fiftieth reunion of her class, she donated Adger's books to Wellesley College and, as so often happens in the case of many important black memorabilia and book collections, it was originally scattered among the other volumes in the college library.

Many black bibliophiles and collectors are familiar with horror

Robert Mara Adger (1837–1910), a notable bibliophile, was also a businessman and political activist. A native of Charleston, South Carolina, the young Adger moved with his family to Philadelphia, Pennsylvania, where he began a successful career as a post office worker and pursued many activities to improve the status of African Americans. He organized the important Afro-American Historical Society in 1897, where he maintained efforts to preserve materials on black history. (Courtesy Dorsey Collection, Manuscripts Department, Moorland-Spingarn Research Center, Howard University, Washington, D.C.)

stories of collections of memorabilia, books, and papers of important black political and literary figures that have been thrown away, burned, or scattered at their deaths. Adger's books were at first dispersed among the volumes at Wellesley College, and it was not until a couple of decades later that their importance was realized and an attempt was made to recall those that were still available. Today, fortunately, although a few volumes have been lost over the years, most are housed separately at Wellesley College in the Rare Book Room.

William H. Dorsey, another of these Philadelphia bibliophiles, had a private museum in his house. Dorsey was very wealthy and was able to devote three or four rooms to this museum. An article in *The Colored American* of 1903 described Dorsey's collection as "without exception the most remarkable collection of books, data, clippings and curios concerning the Negro race in the world." There was also William Carl Bolivar, whose catalog, published in 1914 shortly before he died, listed over one thousand items. Jacob C. White, Jr., was less well known than the other bibliophiles but a most remarkable character—in many ways possibly the most important of all. White was the secretary of many black organizations in Philadelphia for many decades in the latter part of the nineteenth century and into the twentieth century. And for every organization of which he was secretary, he assiduously collected all the documents that came within his possession. Today one of our major sources of information concerning many of these bibliophiles of Philadelphia is the Leon Gardner Collection in the Historical Society of Pennsylvania, a collection based overwhelmingly on documents collected by Jacob C. White, Jr.[1] These are but a few examples of the many individuals who built private collections and collaborated on building institutional collections as well.

These same bibliophiles, men and women, organized the earliest reading rooms and library companies among black people in Philadelphia dating back to the 1820s. Usually, these library companies and reading rooms also served as areas where books were collected. As a result, bibliophiles and collectors literary societies were formed. One of the prime functions of these literary societies was the collection and preservation of rare books by and about black people. One bibliophile who exemplifies this pattern is Adger, who simultaneously built his own private collection and donated books to the Banneker Literary Institute's collection as well.

In 1897 these Philadelphia bibliophiles founded the first historical society, the first narrowly defined historical society among African Americans, that was known as the American Negro Historical Society of Philadelphia. This historical society had as one of its main purposes developing a collection of rare books and artifacts concerning the history of black people in North America and the world. These same bibliophiles contributed resources to the American Negro Historical Society collection.

These bibliophiles were so fond of books and books represented such a large part of their lives that they built collections in just about every kind of organization with which they were involved. Often, they donated rare books to the most unlikely organizations and institutions. For example, a very important repository for Adger's rare books at one point was a home for aged and infirmed colored persons in Philadelphia. I even came across a reference to a Citizen's Republican Club, a Republican party club in 1896, which as an adjunct to its Republican party political activity built up a collection of rare books. So it seems as though any organization in which these people were involved at some point in time became yet another avenue of book collecting activity.

A GROWING NETWORK

These bibliophiles, of course, were not confined to Philadelphia. Philadelphia simply happened to be one of the most active centers of activity among black bibliophiles. From this city an incredible network of like-minded people stretched all the way along the Northeast Coast and even to areas further afield. There developed a network of black bibliophiles who exchanged information and visits and who corresponded for decades. During my research, I've examined the correspondence of some of these bibliophiles. Arthur Schomburg was based in New York, but was a regular visitor to Philadelphia. In terms of where to look to find rare books, Schomburg would get contacts from people like Bolivar. The correspondence between these two men is now housed in the Schomburg Collection in New York City, and it was there I saw one of the last letters from Bolivar to Schomburg dated a few weeks before Bolivar died in 1914.

Daniel Alexander Payne Murray was another of the major bibliophiles based in Washington, D.C., who was very closely linked to the bibliophiles in Philadelphia and in other cities. Murray was a cousin of William Carl Bolivar and was an assistant librarian at the Library of Congress. Murray worked for many years on what was to be a massive six-volume collection known as *Murray's Historical and Biographical Encyclopedia of the Colored Race Throughout the World: Its Progress and Achievements from the Earliest Period Down to the Present Time, Embracing Twenty-Five Thousand Biographical Sketches of Men and Women of the Colored Race in Every Age,* etc. That is not the complete title; it is lengthier and even more explicit.

WHY DID THEY COLLECT?

What was the motivation of these bibliophiles, what were the reasons for this incredible book collecting activity? First, they collected books to counter the pseudo-scientific racism that was so prevalent during that time, when so-called scholars and writers were claiming that black people were by nature inferior, that a black person could not be found who could comprehend geometry, that black people could memorize by rote but could not reason. At a time when that type of gobbledygook was taught in the best universities in the world as accepted truth, the black bibliophiles took it upon themselves to refute such arguments.

One of the ways they could refute those arguments was not only by collecting books, but by collecting books that showed that, far from black people not having been civilized before Europeans got to Africa in the era of the slave trade, black people had in fact been the first civilized people on this planet. So the early bibliophiles were very interested in books dealing with the history of Africa in Egyptian times, in Nubian times. The first historians of Afro-America very often went back for their sources to the Bible, with its references to Ethiopia's greatness, to Herodotus the Greek, with his unbiased accounts of the greatness of black people in Egypt and in other parts of the ancient world. Thus the black bibliophiles had a very political purpose for their book collecting.

A fine illustration of Rev. Peter Williams by Patrick Reason from the
Dorsey Collection. Rev. Williams (1780?–1840), a clergyman and abolitionist, was an opponent of the American Colonization Society's efforts to
return American-born blacks to Africa. Born in New Brunswick, New
Jersey, Williams helped to organize an early African American Episcopal
congregation, which became the St. Philips African Church. In 1826, he
was the second African American ordained into the priesthood of the
Episcopal Church. Williams was one of six African American managers of
the American Anti-Slavery Society when it was organized in 1833. (Courtesy Dorsey Collection, Manuscripts Department, Moorland-Spingarn Research Center, Howard University, Washington, D.C.)

Another goal was to provide a body of information for posterity.
These early black bibliophiles set about their task in a very deliberate
and self-conscious way in order to provide contemporary blacks, their
posterity, with a record of which we could be proud and with
documentation that we could use to further our struggle in our day.
In the black bibliophiles' writings, there are self-conscious references
by these bibliophiles that support the conclusion that the bibliophiles
did collect those books so that their children, coming after them and

their children's children would be enlightened and would be inspired by their struggles and the struggles of those who came before them. Another reason the bibliophiles collected books was to correct the record of American history, to rescue what John Henrik Clarke likes to call "the missing pages of American and world history," introducing into the textbooks the contributions of black people all over the world.

Yet another reason for their collecting was to restore, perhaps even initiate, an "African consciousness," an African perspective on black history. The writings of these early bibliophiles stressed very

This is one of Rev. Peter Williams's letters in which he described the burning of the National Theater and three churches, as well as the destruction of Dr. Brown's books and furniture. (Courtesy Dorsey Collection, Manuscripts Department, Moorland-Spingarn Research Center, Howard University, Washington, D.C.)

consciously that black history included Africa and the Caribbean and wherever else black people lived. The interests of these bibliophiles transcended those of the North American continent, and these bibliophiles were involved in political activities of an African nature, including the various immigration projects and back to Africa movements. Like all black historians and intellectuals who have had The Race at heart, these bibliophiles collected books to instill pride and to provide hope for future generations. Because many of our political leaders have been so fond of saying, as Marcus Garvey said, "Blacks were once great and we can be great again."

By knowing that we were once great we would hopefully be provided the inspiration to strive for greatness again. Robert Mara Adger summed up this motivation in 1904 when he said during a speech,

> We want the newspapers, the churches and the parents to tell their children what our past condition was, and about those dear people who are dead and gone, of the sacrifices they made in our behalf and the grand opportunities [we] are now offered.[2]

This is a most noble statement. There is no more noble purpose for collecting books than to want future generations to know "what our past condition was and about those dear people who are dead and gone of the sacrifices they made in our behalf and the grand opportunities we are now offered."

The reasons for collecting books, then, were not only academic; they were also highly political. These books were being collected with a view to uplifting a downtrodden race of people and because these bibliophiles were so highly political it stands to reason that they would have been active in purely political organizations as well. I mentioned previously that there was hardly a black race uplift organization in Philadelphia for half a century or more that Robert Adger was not involved in, and the same is true for that coterie of black bibliophiles of which he was a part. There were numerous organizations and ad hoc committees of all kinds with which these bibliophiles were involved. During the Civil War there were ad hoc committees to recruit black soldiers. There were ad hoc committees to sponsor lectures by persons like Frederick Douglass, Frances Ellen Watkins Harper, and William Lloyd Garrison; these were the kinds of people who came to town to give lectures. During the Spanish-American

War there was an ad hoc committee to bring relief to sick and wounded African American and Cuban soldiers. Every year on August first West Indian Emancipation Day was celebrated. After 1863 the Emancipation Proclamation on January first was celebrated, and so on.

One of the political organizations that these bibliophiles were involved in was the Pennsylvania State Equal Rights League, founded in 1865. Almost all of these bibliophiles were very active in the Republican party and were such loyalists that they actually made it a condition precedent for membership in some of the other organizations—one had to be a Republican to be a member of some of the other organizations. There was the Social, Civil and Statistical Association of Colored People of Pennsylvania, founded in 1860. There was even a baseball club, The Pythian Baseball Club, founded in 1866. In fact, there was a flourishing black baseball league organized on an informal basis in the Northeast area from Washington, D.C., up to about maybe Connecticut or so in the 1860s. One club would challenge another, and the host club would provide entertainment and refreshments. The club members would bring along their wives and children and they would stay for a weekend. There would be picnics, they would play their games, and so on. Imagine, these bibliophiles even had time to organize a baseball club! Even the names of the baseball clubs exemplified the political nature of the activity. Even in play they couldn't get around the overriding purpose of uplifting the race; names like Excelsior, L'Ouverture (Toussaint L'Ouverture)—these were the types of names that the friends of these black bibliophiles selected for their baseball clubs.

In 1904 the bibliophiles organized the Philadelphia Association for the Protection of Colored Women, an organization that later became one of the component parts of the National Urban League. They were also involved in all the important African American historical societies that followed the earliest pioneer societies for two or three decades thereafter. For example, there was the American Negro Academy, which even though it may not normally be considered a historical society, nevertheless, fulfilled many of the functions of a historical society in which members of the Philadelphia bibliophiles circle were involved. There was the Negro Society for Historical Research, founded by John Edward Bruce and Arthur Schomburg at Yonkers, New York, in 1911, of which William Carl Bolivar and other bibliophiles were corresponding members. There was the Association for the Study of Negro [now Afro-American] Life and History, founded by Carter G. Woodson, in 1915. Here again some of the members of this Philadelphia circle of bibliophiles were involved in that organization as well.

Some of the members of the circle were even involved in the Universal Negro Improvement Association (UNIA) of Marcus Garvey, an organization that one does not normally think of as a historical society as well as a movement. Nevertheless, the UNIA, a mass political organization, the largest that black people have ever produced, was also among other things a kind of historical society, too. As an organization, it had a tremendous impact on popularizing black history. In 1920, the UNIA's famous "Declaration of Rights of the Negro People of the World" called for black history to be taught to black children in school.

It is clear that books for these Philadelphia bibliophiles were much more than leather bindings and first editions. To be sure, they were interested in these technical aspects of the bibliophile's concern. I have read too many letters exchanged between people who were collectors, such as Bolivar and Schomburg, not to know the joy they felt when they came upon a book that was a first edition, a book that was rare, that was bound in sheepskin or what have you, and that was in mint condition. However, books for them were, in the words of the Reverend Henry L. Phillips, "books that tell of the achievements of the race. Books not to fill shelves but books to fill the mind with useful race doings."

NOTES

1. Tony Martin, "Introduction," Wendy Ball and Tony Martin, *Rare Afro-Americana: A Reconstruction of the Adger Library* (Boston: G.K. Hall and Co., 1981), 25.
2. Ibid, 31.

ARTHUR ALFONSO SCHOMBURG (1874–1938), BLACK BIBLIOPHILE AND COLLECTOR

Elinor Des Verney Sinnette

An important objective of "Black Bibliophiles and Collectors: A National Symposium" was to pay tribute to those pioneer black men and women who devoted a lifetime, often at great personal sacrifice, to collecting books and other materials to document the history of their race. Those men and women were faced with the historical imperative of black self-definition and regarded their bibliophilia as a mission, a commitment to a social cause. Collecting for them was not a "delightful diversion," nor did they conform to the general description of bibliophiles "who buy what they like because they like it or buy what appears to be the class of books most likely to appreciate in value."[1] These pioneer black collectors existed in a society that not only denied their humanity but seemed skeptical about their ability to achieve. Consider a few titles of "scientific" works of their time— Charles H. McCord, *The American Negro as a Dependent, Defective and Delinquent* (Nashville: Benson Printing Company, 1914); Robert Bennett Bean, "Some Racial Peculiarities of the Negro Brain," *American Journal of Anatomy*, September 1906; Marion J. Mayo, *The Mental Capacity of the American Negro* (New York: Science Press, 1916).

When I researched Arthur Alfonso Schomburg's life, I found two typewritten sheets among his papers bearing the words of historian Hubert Howe Bancroft: "The [Negro] is too incompetent and un-

Elinor Des Verney Sinnette, chief librarian at the Moorland-Spingarn Research Center, is the author of *Arthur Alfonso Schomburg, Black Bibliophile and Collector*.

reliable . . . as a citizen . . . he is an unmitigated nuisance and judging from the past he will remain so." On the second sheet, referring to blacks, Bancroft is quoted: "However learned he may become, however lofty his ideals or how high his aspirations, he must wear the badge of ignorance and servitude, he and his children, forever. God hath made him so. We do not need the Negro for any purpose and never shall."[2]

Arthur Schomburg's response, handwritten in bold letters at the bottom of the second sheet, was "where are our Negro historians, our defenders who have let Bancroft commit such a dastardly crime against the Negro race?" Schomburg was outstanding among his fellow bibliophiles. His search for his own identity led him to become a foremost collector of books and other materials to document the history of people of African descent. During his personal search, Schomburg became a self-trained historian and a chronicler of black history. As curator of a special collection at Fisk University and later as curator of his own collection in the New York Public Library, he shared his knowledge and material resources with scholars and the general public. The avid search for his heritage, roots, and heroes began in his youth and continued into adult life with a passion and intensity that soon propelled him to become an acknowledged master of his subject.

SCHOMBURG'S EARLY YEARS

Arthur Schomburg was born in San Juan, Puerto Rico, on January 24, 1874, one year after slavery had been abolished on the island. Records in San Juan reveal that his mother, Mary Joseph, described as a *soltera* (unmarried), *lavandera* (washer woman), was from St. Thomas, Virgin Islands. His father may have been one Carlos Schomburg, a German merchant. The circumstances of Arturo Schomburg's early life in Puerto Rico are hazy. We know, however, that he grew up in a society where personal wealth, color, and religion were major determinants of one's status. As the son of a black, unmarried laundress, Arturo's experiences as a child may have well been so unpleasant as to account for his seldom mentioning that period of his life.

In an interview with Gustavo Urrutia, journalist with the leading Cuban newspaper *Diario de La Marina*, Schomburg revealed that he became interested in searching out his roots and heroes because:

> in Puerto Rico there were literary clubs for young people and I belonged to one of those clubs. History was a favorite topic and the whites spoke with much pride about the historical deeds of their ancestors.[3]

In order to match his white companions' stories, young Arturo began to seek out the history of black people throughout the Caribbean. The Haitian revolution captured his imagination and Toussaint L'Ouverture became one of his early heroes.

Schomburg was to be closely involved in revolutionary activity himself as he left Puerto Rico and went to live with his maternal grandparents in St. Thomas. It was here that Arturo may have met black exiled revolutionary Ramon Emeterio Betances and quickly identified with the cause of Cuban and Puerto Rican independence.

Young Arturo arrived in New York City on Friday, April 17, 1891. He hoped to continue his education and for awhile harbored dreams of studying medicine. Without family and finances, however, he had to seek employment to support himself. He settled in lower Manhattan and soon was an active member of Las Dos Antillas, an enthusiastic group of revolutionaries who collected funds, medicine, and weapons to aid the Cuban and Puerto Rican independence movement. He was an "activist" and allied himself with those members calling for sending men if necessary to support the cause. When Cuba, Puerto Rico, and the Philippines were ceded to the United States as part of the treaty that ended the Spanish-American War, there was much internal strife and bickering among the leaders of the revolutionary group. Arturo Schomburg's mentor and father figure, Dr. Julio Henna, supported a policy of cooperation with the United States.

Arturo was disappointed and thoroughly disillusioned. He severed all ties with the Puerto Rican community and began to devote full interest to a more universal black struggle. He became Arthur A. Schomburg and lived the rest of his life as a black man, "a Puerto Rican of African descent," although he was fair skinned enough to have been accepted as one of the many southern European immigrants living in New York City. His close friend, author Claude McKay, described him:

In appearance he was like an Andalusian gypsy, olive-complexioned and curly haired, and he might easily have become merged in that considerable class of foreigners who exist on the fringe of the white world. But, because of his African blood, he chose to identify himself with the Aframerican group.[4]

As a black man, Schomburg encountered widespread and blatant racism and segregation in the United States. He found discrimination in churches, hotels, and restaurants. He had many shocking experiences as he traveled throughout the country.

While identifying solidly with black Americans during these early years, Schomburg was becoming a self-educated historian. He was repeatedly turned down for entrance into schools and courses because of lack of papers and certificates attesting to prior school attendance. Consequently, he began to educate himself through buying and reading books of world history, reading and rereading, carefully underlining pertinent phrases and sentences as he went along.

His job as a bank messenger and his Masonic duties absorbed much of his time, but he joined the Men's Sunday Club, founded by his close, old friend, the fiery and formidable John Edward Bruce, known as "Bruce Grit." The meeting's agenda usually included book discussions and considerable debate on racial matters. The club sponsored fund-raising affairs to purchase books, pamphlets, and documents about black history for the group's library.

THE RESEARCH SOCIETIES

Schomburg's propensity for collecting books and documents purposefully and systematically probably began to develop about the time he and Bruce founded the Negro Society for Historical Research in April 1911. In Bruce, Schomburg found a surrogate father who inspired and encouraged him to pursue his avocation as a bibliophile and collector of Afro-Americana. In 1914, sponsored by Bruce, Schomburg joined the American Negro Academy, where he came into further contact with the leading black scholars of his time, W. E. B. Du Bois, Carter Woodson, and Kelly Miller. The objectives and activities of these two societies significantly inspired Arthur Schomburg's preoccupation with collecting the evidence of black history, and their meetings and conferences provided him an arena

John Edward Bruce (1856–1924) was a journalist, lay historian, and bibliophile. Born a slave in Piscataway, Maryland, Bruce had some formal
schooling but was largely self-educated. He founded several newspapers,
including the *Argus* (1879), *Sunday Item* (1880), and *Washington Grit* (1884).
He edited several publications and wrote for more than twenty African
American newspapers. His articles appeared in white newspapers, and in
black newspapers in Africa, Europe, and the Caribbean. He was known as
"Bruce Grit," the title of his column in the *Gazette* of Cleveland and the
New York Age. Bruce and Arthur A. Schomburg organized the Negro
Society for Historical Research in 1911, one of several efforts in the early
twentieth century that had a profound impact on the development of
African American studies and on the preservation of materials document-
ing black history. (Courtesy Prints and Photographs Department, Moorland-Spingarn Research Center, Howard University, Washington, D.C.)

where he could demonstrate his knowledge and be accepted among
the academicians. In 1920 Schomburg mounted an exhibition of his
books at the American Negro Academy's annual meeting in Washington. This was the first of what would become a yearly feature of
the meetings: a display of new acquisitions by black bibliophiles.

Arthur Schomburg sought to hold his own among the university-
educated scholars and professionals of the American Negro Academy.

He shared philosopher Alain Locke's concern that the trauma of the slavery experience would dominate racial thinking. Schomburg together with Locke called on blacks to develop a new awareness of themselves and their culture, agreeing that as Locke stated, "there was no alternative to turning back toward an African past."[5] Schomburg believed it was important to examine both the African roots and the universality of the black man's history. Many of his differences with members of the American Negro Academy stemmed from the Afro-American tendency to go no further back into the past than to slavery and emancipation. Schomburg considered Africa the ancestral homeland of the black race and believed that until black historians accepted this fact and began to research from that continent out into Europe, Asia, and the Americas, their work would be only half complete.

Schomburg regarded the so-called race question or race problem as universal, as he illustrated in one of his presidential addresses before the American Negro Academy, entitled "Racial Outlook from a World Point of View." Another paper delivered in Rankin Chapel at Howard University in 1920 was "The Negro as a Soldier in the Civilization of America," in which he theorized that the struggle of blacks against racism would eventually bring about racial harmony and truly civilize the Western world.

A major concern of his, stemming perhaps from his early snubs in class conscious Puerto Rico, was the contribution of blacks to Spanish culture. His paper "Fragmentary Tribute to Spanish Negro Painters of the School of Seville," discussing Pareja, Gomez, and Jose Campeche, was prepared for the 1923 meeting of the American Negro Academy. Subsequent articles in *Crisis* and *Opportunity* were "Alessandro, First Duke of Florence: The Negro Medici" and "The Negro Brotherhood of Seville."

In May 1925, Schomburg sold his collection of 5,000 books, manuscripts, prints, and realia to the Carnegie Corporation for $10,000. On June 25, 1925, he sailed for Europe to uncover important missing pieces, black history pieces that lay buried in archives there. He wrote the following to his friend John Wesley Cromwell:

> On the eve of my departure for Seville, Spain, I wish to express my sincere regards for the many years we have labored in the vineyard of usefulness to the race. I depart now on a mission of love to recapture my lost heritage.[6]

These busts by Charles Cordier were among the first pieces in the Art and
Artifacts Collection at the Schomburg Center for Research in Black
Culture. They were acquired by Arthur Schomburg during a trip to
Europe in 1926. (Reprinted by permission of Arts & Artifacts Division,
Schomburg Center for Research in Black Culture, The New York Public
Library, Astor, Lenox and Tilden Foundations)

Although Schomburg contributed diligently to the activities of the
American Negro Academy and was elected president in 1920, he felt
much more comfortable with the members of the Negro Society for
Historical Research, composed of lay historians, many of whom
would, during the Harlem Renaissance, espouse the philosophy of
Marcus Garvey. Arthur Schomburg helped create the race consciousness and race pride engendered during that Harlem Renaissance
period, and Marcus Garvey's message was not lost upon him. Schomburg attended one of Garvey's first public meetings in Harlem and
became a staunch supporter of many of the movement's programs,

although he would later express doubts about the "back-to-Africa" plan. Marcus Garvey impressed him as being "a man of principle whose name will go down in history for integrity in the Negroes' cause." He wrote of the much-maligned Black Star Steamship Company: "The Black Star Line is going to increase its capital from $500.00 to $10,000—then there will be an unusual howl from the doubters—Garvey is the man!"[7]

Schomburg, however, would not risk the criticism of his colleagues of the American Negro Academy and refused John Bruce's request for Garvey to speak before that group, writing to John Wesley Cromwell,

> I've returned to find Bruce's letter pleading for the opportunity to hear Garvey. I have no objection whatever but I am reluctant to bring the matter before the Executive Committee.[8]

Schomburg never denounced Garvey, as many others did, and continued to support his ideals and to assist those in the forefront of the black nationalist movement.

> We cannot forget Marcus Garvey who for several years gave us much inspiration in trying to awaken the dormant mind of our people and in so doing aroused the ire of his enemies. . . . We must admire his indomitable courage.[9]

FINAL YEARS

After a brief tenure as the first curator of a Negro Collection at Fisk University in Nashville, Tennessee, Arthur Schomburg served as curator of his own collection at the 135th Street Branch of the New York Public Library from 1932 until his death in 1938. Harlem was in the throes of depression and as conditions worsened, he became despondent. He grew bitter and disconsolate as certain events caused him to lose faith and to question the effectiveness of his own contribution to the welfare of black people. He felt that the black writers and artists of the Renaissance were no longer revolutionaries and told white anthologist Nancy Cunard she should "not expect to find anything revolutionary or critical in these subjected fellows writings. . . . They have been bought and paid for by white people."[10]

He also recalled that "the so-called Negro artists did not have the courtesy to invite a distinguished Cuban painter to a reception or even for tea. They are so clannish and prejudiced that I have given up having anything to do with them,"[11] he wrote. Further, he disapproved of the rush toward integration and the integrationist policies of the Urban League and the NAACP, favoring separate black organizations and functions where integration was considered unpopular. As a member of the Negro Writers Guild, he supported that group's refusal to admit a white member to its ranks. And when Walter White, executive secretary of the NAACP, informed Schomburg of a centennial celebration honoring Alexander Pushkin and proposed that Negroes be integrated into the whole international "picture," Schomburg replied: "I am willing to abide by the opinion of the majority but I feel that the colored people should have their own exhibition."[12]

Schomburg had to struggle to maintain his position at the library and, deeply hurt, believed that few of the librarians or so-called influential blacks in Harlem were sincerely interested in him. Claude McKay wrote,

> How well he [Schomburg] remembered that when he was first offered the job as curator of the books that he himself had collected, the Negro academicians led by Dr. Du Bois fought against the appointment on the ground that he did not possess a college degree.[13]

In 1937 Schomburg wrote to his friend and fellow bibliophile Wendell P. Dabney of Cincinnati, Ohio,

> I am becoming very doubtful of the Negro finding a place for himself in the next quarter of a century. I believe that the forces that are working in this nation against radicalism are going to converge . . . like pincers and crush our group. We will either be relegated to the . . . sidewalk or back to Africa in the spirit of the philosophy of Marcus Garvey.[14]

Schomburg continued, "I am sick and tired of the conditions that I see every night in Harlem. I am still dreaming of going to the Virgin Islands and spending the remainder of my life in that calm place."[15] Later, he adopted a change in his usually helpful attitude toward writers and scholars:

> I have closed my mouth tighter than a clam and no longer give so

freely of knowledge and information . . . to those who are like a bunch
of vultures on the limb of a tree waiting to pounce down on anything
they can offer a publisher.[16]

By 1938, Schomburg's health was deteriorating but he continued to
plan speaking engagements and meetings. Shortly before an event
he was looking forward to attending, he developed a dental infection
that warranted having a tooth extracted. He became ill and failed to
respond to treatment. He died at Madison Park Hospital in Brooklyn
on June 10, 1938.

Looking back over the trials and what must have seemed to him a
string of personal defeats—at Fisk, at The New York Public Library,
in his beloved Harlem—Schomburg might not have called his lifelong
efforts successful. The events and changing attitudes among blacks
of the 1960s and 1970s would, however, prove how right he was in
his vision and how wrong he would have been in such an assessment
of his achievements. His collection and the Schomburg Center for
Research in Black Culture on 135th Street in Harlem are monuments
to his foresight, wisdom, and courage.

The collection that Schomburg left for posterity is the tangible
expression of his life's work. Seminal as this contribution may be for
future research and scholarship, his intangible efforts are of equal
significance, since they reflect the credo that governed his activities.

NOTES

The following abbreviations for manuscript collections have been used in these
notes: MSRC, Moorland-Springarn Research Center, Howard University, and SCRBC,
Schomburg Center for Research in Black Culture. All quotations from Alfonso
Schomburg letters, *Diario de la Marina*, and *The New York Age* are reprinted by
permission of Rare Books, Manuscripts & Archives Section, Schomburg Center for
Research in Black Culture, The New York Public Library, Astor, Lenox and Tilden
Foundations.

1. George Sargent, "Modern Tendencies in Book Collecting," *Book Selling and Book
Buying, Aspects of the Nineteenth-Century British and North American Book Trade*, ed. Richard
G. Landon, ACRL Publications in Librarianship, 40 (Chicago: American Library
Association, 1978), vii.

2. Hubert Howe Bancroft, *Retrospection, Political and Personal* (New York: Bancroft
Co., 1912), 367.

3. Gustavo E. Urrutia, "Schomburg" Havana, Cuba *Diario de la Marina* (November
2, 1933).

4. Claude McKay, *Harlem: Negro Metropolis* (New York: E. P. Dutton, 1940), 140. By the kind permission of Hope McKay Virtue.

5. Alain LeRoy Locke, "The Question of a Race Tradition," Typescript, 1911, Locke Papers, MSRC, Washington, D.C.

6. Arthur Schomburg to John Wesley Cromwell, June 1 1926, box 24-2, folder 31, Cromwell Family Papers, MSRC, Washington, D.C.

7. Schomburg to Cromwell, undated, box 24-2, folder 32, Cromwell Family Papers, MSRC, Washington, D.C.

8. Schomburg to Cromwell, Oct. 27, 1921, box 24-2, folder 32, Cromwell Family Papers, MSRC, Washington, D.C.

9. Arthur A. Schomburg, "Negroes in the League of Nations," *New York Age*, September 4, 1935.

10. Schomburg to Nancy Cunard, June 9, 1936, Schomburg Papers, SCRBC, New York, New York.

11. Schomburg to Caterina Jarbaro, June 9, 1936, Schomburg Papers, SCRBC, New York, New York.

12. Walter White to Schomburg, October 23, 1936 and Schomburg to White, October 26, 1936, SCRBC, New York, New York.

13. Wayne Cooper, ed., *The Passion of Claude McKay, Selected Poetry and Prose, 1912-1948*, (New York: Schocken Books, 1973), 302.

14. Schomburg to Wendell P. Dabney, August 19, 1937, Schomburg Papers, SCRBC, New York, New York.

15. Ibid.

16. Schomburg to Dabney, April 29, 1938, Schomburg Papers, SCRBC, New York, New York.

ON COLLECTORS,
THEIR CONTRIBUTIONS TO THE
DOCUMENTATION OF THE BLACK PAST

Robert Hill

EARLY BIBLIOPHILES

In the process of researching the life of Marcus Garvey, I found one of the most notable features about him: the degree to which Garvey's career and the history of the Garvey movement intersect with some of the most important work in African American bibliography. One of the first people with whom Garvey came into contact here in the United States—indeed, new evidence that we have turned up suggests that this was the man who gave Garvey the idea for a black merchant marine line in late 1918 that would become the Black Star Line—was Charles C. Seifert, one of the most renowned of the early black bibliophiles and pioneers in the recovery of African-American history. Seifert was a member of the original New York division of the Universal Negro Improvement Association, UNIA. Then there was the resident black radical of Harlem, the father of black radicalism in Harlem—there were really two fathers, John E. Bruce and the distinguished West Indian bibliophile and autodidact Hubert H. Harrison. Harrison was one of the associate editors of *The Negro World* newspaper and was the major innovator in that band of black street orators—that band of black street historians, because that's what they really were. They took history into the streets in Harlem in 1917. Then of course we have the esteemed Professor William H. Ferris, the second editor of *The Negro World* and the compiler of that

Robert Hill is the editor of the multivolume work, *The Marcus Garvey and Universal Negro Improvement Association Papers*, Berkeley: University of California Press, 1983–.

encyclopedic two volume work, *The African Abroad*. There were numerous admirers of Garvey's work—for example, Arthur A. Schomburg and, in Washington, D.C., John Wesley Cromwell—so that Garvey's history seemed to me to be creating a space, creating an environment in which much of the accumulated work in the field of black historical research was now able to empty its riches unofficially. One reason *The Negro World* is such a rewarding experience to read is that, over and above Garvey's own speeches and editorials, which were included, it contains a mass of very vibrant information about the doings of the race in all parts of the world.

DOCUMENTING BLACK RADICALISM

The editing of the Marcus Garvey and UNIA's papers gave me a rare and privileged vantage point from which to assess the possibilities and needs of documenting the origins and the development of black radicalism in America in the first half of the twentieth century. This experience of preparing the Garvey and UNIA papers for a selected edition taught me a great many lessons about pursuing this particular brand of history. It has taught me that the pitfalls are many and severe to the unwary investigator, but it has also taught me that the joy and exhilaration of discovering long-buried and unsuspected aspects of black life in America, Africa, and the Caribbean are unparalleled.

My experience has not been easily acquired, nor can it be easily summarized and passed on as a ready formula for others to repeat. Each historical project is unique. The writing of history, in particular the collective historical experience of political resistance on the part of black people, always entails the reinvention and the reinterpretation of concepts and methodologies that the historian has grasped, made assumptions about, and then called politics, history, masses, struggle. Not the least of all, the very status of the concept of history in the conscious estimation of those who have been responsible for actually making it has to be rethought, as we encounter the experience of the people who made the history. Even this exciting harvest, however, has merely underscored for us historians the critical need to exchange perspectives with other scholars working in the fields of African American history and the history of black popular movements.

This urgency arises from the fact that a particular and highly significant kind of black history, namely the black search for radical solutions to the condition of racial oppression in America, is fast disappearing. To the extent that no people can ever, in truth, lose their history since their history must always live in the collective, accumulated ways of being, knowing, seeing, and reflecting what historians today call mentalities—to this extent we can be assured that people themselves, black people, are the essential guarantors and guardians in their most intimate being of their collective past, and that is what the importance of folklore and research into folk consciousness of black people really signifies.

Humanity is always the poorer for loss that comes with the destruction of even the smallest part of any people's recorded past. The past of black radical struggle for freedom in America is each year—each day—being steadily lost as more and more of the original documentation disappears through the despoliation of black life, the breakdown of our material culture and our instruments of living, indeed the very foundation of memories and motives. This is my view, one that has been arrived at not by any abstract and philosophical search for some ultimate vindication, but arrived at by concretely and daily witnessing the ease with which our people's history has been destroyed and continues to be destroyed. The precious vestiges of what still survives in the documentary record and its possible disappearance make me feel that massive retrieval of what survives must be carried out as a matter of the highest historiographical priority. I cannot see how we can continue to have any respect for ourselves and the black unborn, for black people today, yesterday, and tomorrow, and for history, and not admit the pressing urgency of this task.

The writing of black history, whether of the experience of black radicalism or the experience of black acceptance, cannot come to fruition in the midst of this continuing wholesale vitiation of the most simple knowledge of who did what, when, with whom, against whom, why, for whom, and with what consequence. What I'm arguing for is the need to see black history being able to be carried on or to become equipped for its own special tasks without a more exacting knowledge than we have presently of all the other related and interacting historical parts. Indeed, black radicalism, the study of black radicalism, is not an end in itself; it is merely a point of entry into the totality of black history. And to try to keep them separate—black resistance or black acceptance—cannot be done without harming the essential record of our people.

But the real reason for my growing sense of urgency stems from the simple fact that in trying to document the phenomenon of popular radicalism among black Americans, we have been forced daily to peer into (it would, indeed, be more accurate to say to strain at peering into) the vast empty spaces for which there's still no reliable information or to search for verifiable data to try to describe and explain a multitude of occurrences that our documents present. We are dealing here not with the genuinely obscure, such as what historians experience in attempting a reconstruction of peasant revolts. We are not dealing with the futilism or the precise cultural provenance of transplanted African captives enslaved and transported to the Americas. We are dealing here with the most straightforward particulars of twentieth-century lives, albeit black lives, such as correct name spelling, birth and death dates, occupation, group membership, familial lineage, etc. But since we are dealing with, above everything else, the experience of black people, we are always awakened to the fact that nothing is straightforward about any of our experience. How can we now try to resolve the question of this fundamental gap in coming to know the past, even the most recent past? What is there in documenting black radicalism that can enable us to part the veil and to reenter the once lived but shrouded world of black folks?

It is my belief that black people have always penetrated their own self-protective veil most knowingly whenever they have engaged this brutal society at its most recalcitrant—at the deepest level of denial—and thereupon found it necessary to transcend themselves as black people by radicalizing the terms on which they speak, on which they think, and upon which they organize. The precise and careful study and documentation of those radicalizing moments in black history possess the potential for us to breach a way into and through the many thick layers of black anonymity. The period of black radical history with which I am most familiar concerns the period of extraordinary eruption of black racial consciousness during and immediately following World War I.

Marcus Garvey's movement, the UNIA, was but one, indeed the most resonant and influential, but still only one among a whole constellation of radical, political stimulations in what was a rapidly changing black community here in America, in the Caribbean, Central America, and in Africa. The reconstruction of the historical Garvey phenomenon ultimately necessitates the exploration of the general phenomenon of simultaneous black movements in their most diverse milieu. Indeed, we might say that Garveyism represents a true bridge between the most inarticulate experience of the black masses on the one hand and the relatively more articulate ideas of the radical black intelligentsia. This gives us a sort of historical meeting point by which to view the social and intellectual history of the black community both from above and from below and to do so all within a single glance.

Thus far, we historians have been most concerned to document the rhetoric and the sources of the ideas of the street orators who emerged on Lenox Avenue in Harlem. But more and more I come to wonder about the history of the people who were listening to these orators. Today, although we have a history of the Harlem Renaissance, we have no history of the audience that presented itself to the intelligentsia, to the artistic elite of the Renaissance. Indeed, the same people who listened to Marcus Garvey, who listened to Hubert H. Harrison, W. A. Domingo, and A. Phillip Randolph while on Lenox Avenue, strolling between soapboxes, picking up something here, picking up something there, and moving on, are the same people who moved on later that night to a dance, to their lodges, or to some other important black activity. When they heard Garvey and Harrison and the others they also were coming from somewhere—probably work. The history of the audience is what's missing in the history of black radicalism, the history of the audience that will tell us how they differentiated between what Randolph said and what Garvey said.

In oral interviews with people who lived through these experiences, I have found what the people tell you is entirely different from what a historian, researcher, or scholar brings to the subject or a historian, researcher, or scholar always thought. I always say to my students, "Listen to what the people tell you. It's when you don't listen to what the people tell you that you are most likely to go astray." But listening to the people is not easy. You have to learn how to listen.

Studying the birth of twentieth-century black radicalism within the historical interstices of American war mobilization between 1917 and 1919 has also allowed historians, as an offshoot, to begin to really appreciate and integrate this awareness into a larger and surer perception of the historical relationship that exists between the phenomenon of patriotism during a war and black nationalism at its most outspoken. This relationship is crucial; this relationship between patriotism in war, the demand that America makes on black people to offer themselves to fight in its wars, and the precipitation of a definition of our interests. As Muhammed Ali once said, "No Viet Cong ever called me Nigger." The precipitation of that definition is indeed the source, at its most outspoken, of black nationalism in America. This is the transforming variable in the emergence of all black radicalism and black nationalism from the time of the American war of secession up to the very middle of the twentieth century. And that's one reason why to offer a definition of what black interest is becomes very dangerous still, because those definitions impinge on the national agenda insofar as the definition of America's war aims are concerned. Black people are dangerous. However, now those black nationalist voices are at times faint ones, not due to any incapacity on the part of their speakers, but due rather to our demoralization, our historical and continuing neglect of black history, a neglect that imposes a harsh and relentless necessity for us to discover adequate procedures to open up the process of historical rearticulation.

MANUSCRIPT COLLECTIONS

At a modest estimate, my colleagues and I have identified, through the period of 1917 to 1927, slightly more than 100 black radicals—however the perimeters of that elusive phenomenon are defined—and yet there presently exist, and I stand open to correction, manuscript collections of no more than nine such radical figures: John E. Bruce, W. E. B. Du Bois, Carter G. Woodson, William Pickens, Frank Crosswaith, Mary Church Terrell, Langston Hughes, Claude McKay, and now Marcus Garvey. Eventually, to be added to the list will be the papers of Asa Phillip Randolph, but it is not expected that the Randolph Collection will be processed and opened by the Manuscript Division of the Library of Congress for some time to come. I congratulate Howard University and the Moorland-Spingarn Research Center for acquiring the Paul Robeson Archives. The Robeson Archives are a tremendous addition to our knowledge of early twentieth-century black history. But whichever way we count it, the

Marcus Mosiah Garvey (1887–1940) was a fiery ora-
tor and organizer in 1914 of the Universal Negro
Improvement and Conservation Association and African Communities League, known popularly and ab-
breviated as the UNIA. A committed black nationalist, Garvey had a tremendous impact during his
lifetime and is revered for his plans to better the
plight of African peoples. A Jamaican by birth,
Garvey and his organization had their greatest impact in the United States. Although his grandiose
plans were unsuccessful, Garvey's successful organization of a mass movement linking blacks in the
United States, Africa, the Caribbean, and other areas
of the diaspora is a continuing legacy. (Courtesy
Prints and Photographs Department, Moorland-Spingarn Research Center, Howard University, Washington, D.C.)

number of black historical figures for whom manuscript collections are currently available or are likely to become available is less than nine percent of the cohort of identifiable black radicals for the entire interwar period.

NEWSPAPERS AND JOURNALS

When we turn to examine the availability of original publications we find an even more limiting picture. For example, in the case of early twentieth-century black newspapers, which sometimes contain the most valuable and only accessible information of the thought and action of diverse individuals and black communities, the loss from destruction has been colossal. In 1923 the National Negro Press Association (NNPA) estimated that there were about 300 Negro newspapers published in the United States. This figure was more than double the 141 black newspapers that were earlier reported for the period from 1916 to 1919, so that between 1919 and 1923 the number of black newspapers published in this country doubled. Unquestionably, there must have been a demand for these newspapers. The sheer number of these newspapers forces historians to ask the question, "What was the readership of these newspapers? Do we know anything about the people who read black newspapers?" However, of the over 300 newspapers published in 1923 the NNPA report said that eighteen were "the better publications," and further, "the reason for this is that they each have a large circulation in the north and west and they wielded a large influence." How many of these eighteen "better publications" can we find today? Only six can be found!

The really appalling figure is that no more than a total of twelve black newspapers for the entire period can be located today, a figure that represents 4.33 percent at most of the more than 300 newspapers published in the early 1920s. The question must be asked, what kind of history is being written when the basic documentary pool of data from which a historian or researcher is drawing constitutes no more than roughly four percent of what existed? However, there is one saving factor in this critical shortage for documenting the emergence of black consciousness in the postwar period—that factor is the newspaper clipping collections that were developed by Monroe Work at Tuskegee Institute and at Hampton Institute [now Hampton University]. Although there are a number of other smaller newspaper collections at most of the black institutions, these two collections, at Hampton and at Tuskegee, are the most extensive. There is a problem in using the collections, however, as neither of them is indexed and each carries only the original subject classification to guide the researcher. Over the years the classifications are changed so that one may find a subject under one classification but then it disappears and sometimes you have to look very hard to see where it's been moved. Whether because black radicals edited them or because they embodied a good deal of radical utterances, the picture grows even dimmer when we turn from the general to the particular, from newspapers of general interest to journals and newspapers particularly relevant to reconstructing black radical thought and activity in the post World War I period. Of the nineteen radical black publications that we have identified, three still cannot be found: *The Christian Recorder, The Clarion*, and *Our Boys and Girls*. Only two of these nineteen, *The Crisis* and *The Messenger*, are available in complete runs. Of the remaining fourteen publications, only very small and partial collections of their issues can be found. Indeed, the mere recovery of these very scattered issues, no matter how partial they are, would represent, in the view of most researchers, a major breakthrough. Garvey's *Negro World*, the official organ of the UNIA, began publication in August of 1918, but the only thing resembling a coherent run of that newspaper is available only from February to March of 1921. In other words, the first two and a half years of the crucial history of the UNIA in America, extending from the formative period through the period of genuine ideological maturation, are represented by a haphazard and disjointed collection of issues numbering less than twenty.

CONCLUSION

What all this means to me is that the study of black radical history must be conducted to an important degree through the prism of sources that require considerable decoding and reaggregation of their data. This aspect of documentation has certain compensating methodological features because it is through the refraction of one radical tendency in the publication of other black radical thought that we can see the interlocking relationship between all of the streams of black radicalism.

The final question that confronts historical research in the area of black radical history is the decision that many of us have to face as to the most appropriate form for the transmission and dissemination of the data we have found, whether it is disseminated in select letter press or microform editions or whether in the form of efficient indicative guides to already assembled collections. Many factors outside of this strict editorial and historiographical process impinge on that ultimate decision; such as the availability of the materials themselves and the decision about even the most primitive form of their communication. Even the most primitive form of their transmission would satisfy many of the existing needs of scholars today. The main thing, therefore, is not really the form of transmission, but the quality that goes into the collection phase, the organization, and the preparation of supporting scholarly apparatuses.

When all has been said and done—when all is done that is within our present knowledge and power to do—always, we are obliged to return to that quintessential principle that I think vindicates our enterprise as historians of black radicalism. It is a principle that we dare not ever forget and still remain true to the trust that we bear. For above all else, our work as historians of the black radical past brings us face to face with the luminous clarity of the voices of those men and women whose hard travail brought us to where we stand today. The history that we produce and that we call the history of black radicalism is no more than a small down payment on our part of the large debt we still owe, and can never fully repay, to the inestimable humanity of those many thousands gone who with tramping feet, aching backs, and through ceaseless intellectual toil have given us today a vision of black freedom in this land, given us a vision of a transformed America that sustains all of us.

PART III

The Development of
Black Public Special Collections

AN OVERVIEW,

INCLUDING THE SPECIAL COLLECTIONS

AT FISK UNIVERSITY

Jessie Carney Smith

BEGINNINGS

Some uninitiated Americans have assumed that black studies and supporting collections began with the advent of the civil rights movement in the 1960s. That is a "civil wrong," for as long as black people have lived they have preserved their history and culture in one form or another. The materials created and preserved may have been in different forms, such as oral or visual, yet these very resources have had an impact on the development of the collections housed in private and public repositories. Discussions eleswhere in this book bring the matter of the anatomy of such collections to the forefront and make moot the issue of why they were founded.

The title of this section, "The Development of Black Public Special Collections," differentiates between those collections that are public and those that are available in private repositories, which the public has at least some right to use. The development of black private collections helped give impetus to the founding of public ones, for such private collections often have become the nucleus around which public collections were built. Frequently, the private collector was the architect for the collections now found in libraries and other centers of learning. For example, materials collected by Langston Hughes, W. E. B. Du Bois, and Carl Van Vechten are well represented among

Jessie Carney Smith is university librarian and professor at Fisk University.

the black research resources in a number of repositories—Atlanta University Center library, Fisk, University of California at Los Angeles, Yale, and elsewhere.

The historical development of special black collections that have been assembled and subsequently housed in American libraries would make interesting study. Doubtless, the patterns of their development would vary, yet one common element in their background would be the sheer love of books, manuscripts, or archives that someone possessed. A second common element would be the insight that the collector had regarding the potential use of these materials to promote scholarship and research. This someone—this great collector—could have been Arthur Spingarn, Arthur Schomburg, W. E. B. Du Bois, Charles F. Heartman, Clarence Holte, or Charles Blockson. Or, the collector could have been one whose name is little known, but who helped to preserve important and currently popular local history collections.

TODAY'S COLLECTIONS

The logical question now is, where are America's black resources? The response—they surround us, they encompass us, they are both far and near. Fortunately for the researcher, however, their bibliographic accessibility today is much more complete than it was just a decade ago. America's black resources may be grouped under as many headings as one will find in the Library of Congress list of subject headings. The resources could be cited alphabetically by donor, by the one around whom the collection is built, by repository, or by geographical area. I have chosen to cite them by geographical arrangement, although I do so with caution. The number of public collections in the black community is well worth the effort of determining where they are and what they contain.

The Northeast

My earlier research on black collections demonstrated that the leading, more popular public collections are in clusters in every region of this nation. The clusters tend to include public libraries, state libraries and archives, and, obviously, those in colleges and universities. The repositories in the District of Columbia deserve special mention because of their numbers and include Howard University's notable Moorland-Spingarn, the Library of Congress, the National Archives, and the more specialized repositories such as those at the Association for the Study of Afro-American Life and History (ASALH).

Elsewhere in the Northeast, some outstanding collections are in New York, where the famous Schomburg Center for Research in Black Culture is located; New Haven, where the James Weldon Johnson Memorial Collection is housed at Yale; and in Pennsylvania, where the notable Charles Blockson Collection is housed at Temple University. Lincoln University (Pennsylvania) should be noted for its outstanding black collection which includes the papers of one of its former students, Langston Hughes.

The Midwest

The cluster in the Midwest includes Oberlin College with its antislavery collection, Northwestern with its African Collection, the Detroit Public Library with its Burton Historical Collection and the E. Azalia Hackley Collection, and the Carter G. Woodson Library of the Chicago library system.

The West

The Western cluster seems to lack the concentration of black collections that is found elsewhere. Nonetheless, the West attracts more than movie stars and gambling casinos. There are, for example, black collections at UCLA. One should also consider UCLA's interest in establishing separate cultural studies programs for ethnic minorities and the development of libraries to support these programs. Other repositories in the West include the Hoover Institution on War, Revolution and Peace and especially the materials on Africa that it collects.

The South

In the South, public black collections are found at the Amistad Research Center in New Orleans, the collections at Duke University, the University of North Carolina's Southern Historical Collection, and the Manuscript Division of the University of Virginia. One or more of these libraries have collected plantation records, other materials on slavery and antislavery and the Underground Railroad, agricultural papers on the production of cotton and tobacco, and materials on the instruction of slaves.

The founding of black colleges, primarily in the South, also led to the collection and development of important resources on blacks. Among these is the collection at Hampton University—a much underpublicized but very rich collection on black Americans and on the Native American who studied there during the 1890s. At Tuskegee University, one finds the Booker T. Washington Collection, excluding those materials that are located in Washington, and the papers of Monroe Nathan Work, whose pioneer *Bibliography of the Negro in Africa and America* insured the preservation of black scholarship. Tuskegee also houses George Washington Carver's collection of papers and the Carver museum.

Collections in the Woodruff Library, Atlanta University Center, include archives and special black materials formerly housed in libraries of the five institutions that form the center. Of special note, however, are the papers of Hoyt Fuller—a fairly recent addition to the center library. Texas Southern University proudly and justly boasts the acquisition of the papers of former Congresswoman Barbara Jordan.

The collections at Fisk University are grouped under specific headings. The headings provide an overview of the richness of our collections. The mark of black bibliophile Arthur Alfonso Schomburg is visible in our collections. His imprint results from Schomburg's service as curator of the Fisk collections in the early 1930s. Arna Bontemps also contributed to the development of Fisk's collections after the Schomburg era. Among our numerous resources are the following groups of materials:

1. The Fisk Archives. Included here are papers of the noted Fisk Jubilee Singers and the papers of noted sociologist Charles S. Johnson, our first black president.
2. Art. In addition to the papers of Harlem Renaissance artist Aaron Douglas, we have the Douglas murals in the administration build-

A bookplate used by the Fisk University Library featuring that university's well-known Fisk Jubilee Singers, who played an important role in raising funds and bringing well-deserved recognition to the school during its concert tours in the United States and abroad. (Courtesy Special Collections Department, Fisk University Library)

ing, folk-type drawings by Winold Reiss, and African drawings (of African types).

3. Literature. Arna Bontemps, Charles Waddell Chesnutt (including his personal library), James Weldon Johnson, Langston Hughes, and Jean Toomer are represented in the collections on black literature.

4. Music. Represented here are the papers of composer John W.

The Fisk Jubilee Singers were for many years well-known ambassadors for Nashville's Fisk University. They traveled widely in the United States and abroad and introduced many audiences to African American music traditions. Although the group's membership changed, it remained famous for the high quality of its performances. (Courtesy Prints and Photographs Department, Moorland-Spingarn Research Center, Howard University, Washington, D.C.)

   Work III, the George Gershwin Memorial Collection of Music and Musical Literature, and the W. C. Handy, Thomas Andrew Dorsey, and Scott Joplin collections.

5. Organizations. Fisk has the papers of Sigma Phi Pi and the Julius Rosenwald Fund Archives.

6. Politics and Law. Included here are papers of William Levi Dawson, John Mercer Langston, and noted Nashville civil rights attorney Z. Alexander Looby.

7. Race Relations. Charles S. Johnson and Robert E. Park are among those persons whose collections are at Fisk. Papers of the Race Relations Information Center are also there.

8. Social Issues. Papers of W. E. B. Du Bois and Marcus Garvey are included in this portion of the Fisk Collections.

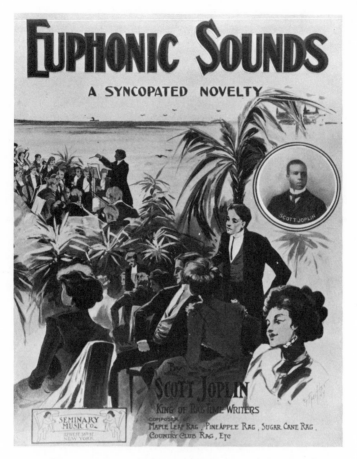

Scott Joplin (1868?–1917) was a composer and pianist who became best known for his magnificent and popular ragtime compositions. A gifted pianist from an early age, Joplin was one of the preeminent composers of his time. His masterpiece, *Treemonisha*, an opera, was rejected by the musical establishment and never performed during his life. Joplin received a posthumous Pulitzer prize for his compositions in 1976, after an astounding rebirth of his music. *Euphonic Sounds* was published in 1909. (Courtesy Music Department, Moorland-Spingarn Research Center, Howard University, Washington, D.C.)

The Lincoln Bible, a hand-tooled volume presented to President Abraham Lincoln by "the loyal coloured people of Baltimore as a token of respect and gratitude," on July 4, 1864, and presented to Fisk University in 1916 by Robert Todd Lincoln. (Courtesy Special Collections Department, Fisk University Library)

9. Women. Among those black women whose papers are at Fisk are Eileen Southern and Naomi Long Madgett.

Miscellaneous Items. Of special significance are the Lincoln Bible (given to Fisk by Robert Todd Lincoln) and a Bible especially edited for slaves. One of our interesting collections is the Effa Manley Collection of blacks in baseball. Fisk also has a black oral history program, and tapes and transcripts from persons interviewed for the program are on file.

CONCLUSION

Libraries, like bibliophiles, may create collections. I dare not close without indicating how Fisk has been able to create black research resources with funds from the National Endowment for the Humanities. Our Learning Library Program, which is in its third year of operation, has enabled us to prepare videotapes, audiotapes, oral history tapes, photographs, and manuscript materials on three topics: the Harlem Renaissance, black music, and black folk culture.

The development and identification of special black collections that are available for public use continue to be subjects for much needed research. The interested researcher could delve deeper into this subject through published guides to these collections and through contact with repositories for the location of unindexed resources. The results would truly benefit scholarship.

THE SCHOMBURG CENTER
FOR RESEARCH IN BLACK CULTURE

Jean Blackwell Hutson

The Schomburg Center for Research in Black Culture is unique among great repositories. Part of the New York Public Library system, it began as the reference section of a community branch library almost sixty years ago. The fact that the center had a community base and support has not always been emphasized in accounts of the center's history and development.

BACKGROUND

In 1925, through the efforts of the branch librarians and a number of concerned black citizens, the Division of Negro Literature, History and Prints was established at the 135th Street Branch of the New York Public Library in Harlem. Bibliophiles John E. Bruce, George Young, Reverend Charles D. Martin, and Arthur Schomburg were joined by artist Louise Latimer and teacher/orator Hubert Harrison to form an advisory committee to librarian Ernestine Rose and her able staff. Together a collection of books and other resources dealing with the history and culture of black people was placed in a separate area of the building and designated as a reference collection.

At this period of history, Negroes (as we were then called) were moving into Harlem from lower Manhattan, the deep South, and the Caribbean and a new, predominately black community was established. The 135th Street Branch Library, situated close to the corner of Lenox Avenue, became a cultural center, as literary, dramatic, and

Jean Blackwell Hutson is the former chief of the Schomburg Center for Research in Black Culture.

The Awakening of Ethiopia, by Meta Warrick Vaux Fuller (1877–1968), is a lifesize statue depicting a black woman emerging from the wrappings of a mummy. It was done in 1921 for the "Making of America Exhibit" in New York and is located in the Schomburg Center for Research in Black Culture. (Reprinted by permission of Art & Artifacts Division, Schomburg Center for Research in Black Culture, The New York Public Library, Astor, Lenox and Tilden Foundations)

artistic programs were sponsored by community groups and held in the library. *The New Negro*, an anthology of black writing edited by Alain Locke in 1925, and the special issue of *Survey Graphic* entitled "Harlem, Mecca of the New Negro" epitomized the Harlem Renaissance, a period of black expression that reverberated within the library as well as within Madame C. J. Walker's famous salon, "The Dark Tower." The Division of Negro Literature, History and Prints sponsored an extensive exhibition of books, manuscripts, and art work highlighting achievements by blacks in these areas. During the opening ceremony, Miss Rose stressed the importance of housing such a collection in a public library, "available equally to scholars, to the man in the street and to school children of all races."

The following year, 1926, the private library of Arthur Alfonso Schomburg was purchased by the New York Public Library with funds obtained from the Carnegie Corporation with the assistance of the Urban League. Mrs. Catherine Latimer, who may have been the first black professional librarian in the New York Public Library System, was the main force in the integration of this valuable collection into the assemblage of black books already housed in the 135th Street library. She was an energetic and talented cataloger who also delighted in receiving and instructing young visitors. In 1932 Arthur Schomburg came to the library as curator of the collection.

Arthur Schomburg, Alain Locke, and the librarian Miss Rose played a dynamic role in Works Project Administration (WPA) sponsored adult education and cultural and artistic programs that took place in the 135th Street library. When I was first employed by the New York Public Library in 1936, a part of the general staff was funded by the WPA and Catherine Latimer supervised them in researching and calendaring manuscripts. From 1932 to 1938, Arthur Schomburg lectured and encouraged a wide range of cultural activities in the community. Following his death in 1938, the Negro Division, renamed in his honor, became the Schomburg Collection.

Dr. Lawrence D. Reddick succeeded Mr. Schomburg as curator and placed an even greater emphasis on the library's participation in community events than his predecessor. Reddick launched a lecture series, set up topical exhibits, and took an interest in the observance of special occasions and the commemoration of significant events in African and African American history. Probably his most successful project was the Schomburg Collection's "Honor Roll in Race Relations," which issued annual awards. During the 1940s, persons named to the Honor Roll considered this one of their greatest achievements. The collection won wide recognition and the enduring friendship of its awardees.

Under Dr. Reddick's leadership, the Schomburg Collection became involved with the activities of the NAACP and the National Urban League. The lecture series it sponsored often featured outstanding black scholars discussing and debating the issues of the day. The theatrical productions staged in the library's auditorium under the aegis of the American Negro Theatre proved to be a training ground for such well-known performers as Frederick O'Neal, Sidney Poitier, and Harry Belafonte. Thus in the 1940s the Schomburg Collection became far more than a reference collection. It was a civic and cultural agency or institution playing an activist role in a community that by that time had become national in scope and varied in interest.

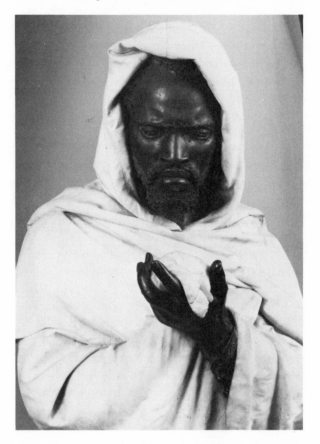

Ira Aldridge as "Othello," by Pietro Calvi, is the signature piece of the Schomburg Center for Research in Black Culture. The bronze and marble bust of the noted Shakespearean thespian was acquired at an auction in New York in 1934 by Arthur Schomburg. (Reprinted by permission of Art & Artifacts Division, Schomburg Center for Research in Black Culture, The New York Public Library, Astor, Lenox and Tilden Foundations)

When Dr. Reddick resigned in 1948, the library administration appointed Dr. Dorothy Williams to succeed him. Although Dr. Williams remained only a few months as curator of the Schomburg Collection, she conducted a survey and reevaluation of the facility's role during that time that resulted in a set of recommendations that ultimately served as guidelines for the collection's growth and development during the following two decades. Dr. Williams suggested that the "activist" stance the facility had assumed under Dr. Reddick be "abandoned" for a more reference and research-oriented posture.

GROWTH AND DEVELOPMENT

I came to the Schomburg to substitute for Dr. Williams when she was granted a six-month leave of absence. I stayed for thirty-two years, leaving only one year to serve as assistant librarian at the University of Ghana, where I developed the Africana library. My first decade at the Schomburg was comparatively peaceful because I concentrated my efforts in processing the four storerooms of acquisitions that had accumulated since the retirement of Catherine Latimer. I was the first one responsible for such matters following the termination of the WPA Project in 1940. In addition, I publicized the contents and activities of the collection to local groups, many of whom were unaware of its rich resources.

The circumstances of Dr. Reddick's resignation alienated some members of the community who had worked closely with him, and I set out to win other users. Fortunately, I had the support of the National Urban League as well as the New York chapter of that organization. Two friends who were most helpful were Dr. Marguerite Cartwright, a teacher at Adelphi and Hunter colleges, and the author Langston Hughes. Hughes began by urging me to sponsor an evening program based on the works of Nicolás Guillén, Cuba's national poet, and Eusebia Cosme, an Afro-Cuban singing and dramatic artist. Translations of Guillén's poetry by Langston Hughes were read. Another outstanding program was based on the book *Selected Poems of Claude McKay* and another on Langston Hughes and Arna Bontemps's *Poetry of the Negro*.

I continually stubbed my toe on the budget problem, which was one of the reasons for Reddick's departure. He had had connections with the General Education Fund, whose grant to the collection had expired, and I tried to obtain another grant from Dr. Channing Tobias, then educational director of the Phelps Stokes Fund. I was greatly chagrined by the manner in which he turned down my request. However, as the result of Dr. Tobias's strongly worded letter to the New York Public Library, I was given an increased budget for the

Schomburg. Up until then the growth of the collection was largely due to gifts, but Dr. Tobias's letter forcefully made the point that it was about time the library purchased the books needed for the Schomburg Collection. Among the important acquisitions that were processed in this period were the papers of the Negro Writers Project, *The Negro in New York*, and the papers of the National Negro Congress.

I recall the turmoil I caused among the staff for having the collection inventoried; such mundane duties had not been performed in twenty years. When the inventory was complete, I had the satisfaction of getting all the holdings in sequential order. At this time the collection was housed on the top floor of the new library building on 136th Street named for poet Countee Cullen in 1950. To enter the Schomburg, one had to climb four steep flights of stairs, a fact that barred Dr. Alain Locke from completing his last work and caused asthmatic attacks in others. Then in 1954 the collection was given quarters in the old 135th Street building, usurping space formerly allotted to the children's collection; the children did the climbing to the second floor of the Countee Cullen building.

Also in 1954 came the historic Supreme Court decision on school desegregation. Much of the research for the legal brief preceding that decision had been prepared in the Schomburg. The small staff had a real sense of participating in that event. But then came the scary suggestion within the New York Public Library Administration that the Schomburg Collection would not be needed any longer because Negro history would be integrated into the general collections!

One friend of the Schomburg, Robert Kingery, who was then chief of the Preparation Division of the New York Public Library, arranged for the G. K. Hall Company to film the catalog of the Schomburg Collection. This was done in spite of the misgivings of the perfectionist cataloger who dreaded having any mistakes so preserved. To the surprise of all concerned, this publication, *The Dictionary Catalog of the Schomburg Collection of Negro Literature and History* (1962), sold to libraries throughout the United States, Europe, and Africa. Mr. Hall had undertaken this publication as a somewhat philanthropic gesture, but was pleased and surprised that it sold.

It didn't do the Schomburg any harm to have the *Dictionary Catalog* available when black studies emerged in the 1960s as a result of the so-called black revolution. Libraries that had seemed unable to afford books purchased the catalog and before long G. K. Hall issued a supplement in 1967 and in 1972.

A dramatic event that I now recognize as typical of my story was the joyful way I entered into the plan to observe the ninetieth birthday of Dr. W. E. B. Du Bois in 1958 . At this period, Du Bois had been indicted by the federal government for failing to register as a Communist under the Alien Registration Act. A bust of Du Bois sculpted by William Zorach was placed in the Schomburg Collection and historian Van Wyck Brooks delivered an appreciative lecture for the celebration. The reading room was jammed with FBI agents watching the Communists, and the Communists watching anti-Communists to such an extent that most of the readers who usually attended such programs were left on the sidewalk. The event was climaxed by a coalition of anti-Communist forces writing threats to cut off contributions to the New York Public Library.

FUNDING CONCERNS

Meanwhile, in March 1971, a corporation was formed by individuals and organizations concerned with the Schomburg Collection's needs and future. Some personal history forms a background for this corporation. The seed for its development was planted in my mind by Dr. Carleton Sprague Smith, who had known Arthur Schomburg and witnessed the collection's early development. He had also participated in fund raising for the Library for the Performing Arts as it developed as a part of Lincoln Center. Dr. Smith visited my flat in Ghana while I was working at the university there in the academic year of 1964–65, and said: "When you come home we'll have to do something about the Schomburg." Sure enough, he did meet with me when I came home in 1965. Then with the help of Whitney Young of the National Urban League (through his friendship with the Rockefeller brothers), I attended the First World Festival of Negro Arts in Dakar, Senegal, in April 1966. My chief intent was to acquire, for the Schomburg, publications I had spied in Dakar when I was on my way down the coast of West Africa going to Ghana in 1964.

Through my friendship with Langston Hughes, who was the center of much admiration in Dakar, along with Leopold Senghor and Amie Cesaire as the historical and literary trio responsible for the festival, I came to the attention of *Ebony* magazine. An *Ebony* staff writer who relied upon the Schomburg Collection for his research was Allen Morrison, who had tried without success to convince *Ebony* editors to run a story on the Schomburg Collection. Not until I was noticed by the *Ebony* representatives at the festival was the Schomburg considered newsworthy. Thus, Ponchita Pierce, with whom I shared the plane traveling overnight to Dakar, wrote the influential story titled "Schomburg's Ailing Collection" in the October 1967 edition of *Ebony*.

Of course, this was also the period in which the concern about black history was stirring college students. During the students' strike at Columbia University, the Harlem community threatened to take over the Schomburg and to make it independent of the New York Public Library: that demand was taken seriously by the library administration.

I may have played a part in arousing concern about the future welfare of the Schomburg because I spoke of the need for an endowment when I was given an award by the Association for the Study of Negro Life and History in February 1966. Dr. Kenneth B. Clark received an award on that same occasion and said, I recall, that "accepting an award for past behavior is making a commitment for the future," and he pledged himself to work to ensure the future of the Schomburg. Earlier, Clark had written in the *Wilson Library Bulletin*, September 1965, an essay on what an inspiration Arthur Schomburg had been to him when as a small immigrant boy he was not permitted to play in the streets of Harlem. He met Schomburg when he ventured upstairs to the third floor of the library, where Schomburg explained to him the significance of the heroes whose pictures adorned the walls and emphasized the fact that one need not be physically tall and large to be heroic.

After this award ceremony, the Schomburg Endowment Fund was established under Dr. Clark's leadership. Members met and raised funds and became involved with yet other groups that met at the Harlem YMCA, discussing what to do about the Schomburg Collection. Out of such discussions there emerged another organization, the Schomburg Corporation, incorporated in March 1971, and concerned about the condition, needs, and future of the Schomburg Collection.[1] The purposes of the Schomburg Corporation were to raise funds for the conservation and preservation of material in the collection, to work toward the construction of a new building that would adequately house the collection, and to solicit new material for the collection.

The Schomburg Corporation helped to obtain a grant from the National Endowment for the Humanities in 1972, and it raised funds to meet the requirements of that grant. The grant continued through June 30, 1974, and was followed by a second and third grant from the NEH for 1974–76 and 1976–78. The corporation, with cooperation from the New York Public Library and interested political figures, secured an award under the Federal Public Works Employment Act of 1976 to give the Schomburg Collection its vitally needed new home.

One little-known aspect of the recent history of the Schomburg is the vital support of the New York State Legislature, which has enabled the Schomburg to maintain longer hours of opening than many other units of the New York Public Library and has substantially augmented funds for staff, acquisitions, and preservation. The first grants in 1973 were largely spearheaded by State Senator Sidney von Luther, but his effectiveness has been continued and even extended by Senator Carl McCall and Assemblyman George Miller, with the support of the Black and Puerto Rican Legislative Caucus.

A national fund-raising campaign by mail, under the leadership of Mrs. Ralph Bunche and Drs. John Hope Franklin and Robert Weaver, raised matching funds for two grants from the National Endowment for the Arts. It initiated an annual fund-raising dinner and produced a quarterly journal mailed to donors and national educational institutions. Today the Schomburg is a living monument to the efforts and concerns of those who helped transfer the private library of Arthur Schomburg to a public center for research in black culture.[2] In addition, 1972 was the year in which the administration of the Schomburg Collection was transferred to the Research Libraries (formerly the Reference Department) of the New York Public Library. The collection was renamed the Schomburg Center for Research in Black Culture and I, the former curator, became the chief. As Stanton Biddle, the center's archivist has said quite aptly, "We gained something and we lost something" by that change.[3] The Schomburg gained professional recognition as a national resource with the January 1972 grant from the National Endowment for the Humanities, which literally gave a new lease on life to much of the Schomburg's holdings by enabling the staff to clear up a cataloging backlog of nonbook materials and a wide range of 89 monographs, 29 archival record groups and 340 titles on microfilm.

In its 1973–74 legislative session, the State of New York provided $250,000 in state aid to the Schomburg Center as a result of legislation introduced by then State Senator Sidney von Luther. Another grant was received for 1974–75. Included in the 1974–75 appropriation were funds for the maintenance and expansion of services and the acquisition, preservation, and restoration of materials and collections, which enabled the center to employ more professional staff.

Late in 1973, the National Cash Register Corporation developed a proposal to convert the extensive vertical file maintained under some 10,000 subject headings to microfiche. The vertical file consisted of clippings from nonblack periodicals, newspaper clippings, broadsides, programs, playbills, leaflets, pamphlets, newsletters, book reviews, typescripts, post cards, menus, and other types of ephemera. This file has been maintained from the beginning of the collection in 1925 up to the present.

The Schomburg Center was designated as one of the Research Libraries of the New York Public Library system. This administrative change provided conservation consultants to the center through the staff of the Conservation Division, and the grant from the National Endowment provided funding for a technical staff that could be trained in the preparation of materials for filming. Meantime, the National Endowment for the Humanities awarded a new two-year matching grant (July 1974–June 30, 1976) to the Schomburg Center, which ensured continued funding for the technical staff. A proposal was drafted, forwarded, and funded by the Ford Foundation for filming the vertical file.

THE NEW BUILDING

The new building, as described by its architect J. Max Bond, Jr., of Bond Ryder Associates,

> was designed to retain the existing Schomburg building, enhance the Lenox Avenue frontage with an art gallery and street trees, provide a

The Schomburg Center for Research in Black Culture (right) is shown with the original Schomburg Center building (left). (Courtesy Art and Artifacts Division, Schomburg Center for Research in Black Culture)

sense of the library's purpose by opening the reading rooms, garden and amphitheatre to public view and provide pleasant workable spaces for those who use the Center.

Three reading areas . . . are housed one above the other in an octagonal drum. . . . This was our way of expressing African tradition in the design element. As an additional reflection of the cultural and also economic links between Africans and African American and because of its beauty, sapele wood imported from West Africa was the material chosen for the shelves and wall paneling of the two major reading rooms. Brick was used for the exterior of the building not only to reflect the materials of most of the nearby buildings but also because the largest proportion of minority workers in the construction trades are masons. And we wanted to ensure their participation in the building's construction.

Simply put, the design and materials are intended to support the purposes of the Schomburg Center itself, which are, as we understand them, to reflect and reinforce the culture and work of African people throughout the world.[4]

This lovely new building provides only for rehousing the archival and library collections. "New Technology for Old Treasures," by James Briggs Murray, in *The Schomburg Center Journal* for Winter 1983, describes the audiovisual documentation that has grown remarkably in its new home. However, the new building was planned to supplement the old 135th Street structure, and that structure remains a challenge to the community and the library to be renovated for proper preservation and display of the art collection and also to provide ample space for lectures and other types of meetings. The basement of that old building was the home of the American Negro Theatre, from which many of our most successful actors graduated. At present, the new building is overused by community activities it was not prepared to house. Book parties and exhibitions are crowded into the archival "search" room, the reference room, the tiny gallery, and the lobby on off-hours. Thus the tradition of serving the community is continued and the need for renewed support is still very great.

NOTES

1. "The Schomburg Corporation," *The Schomburg Center for Research in Black Culture Journal*, 1, no. 2 (Spring 1977), 3. Reprinted by permission of *The Schomburg Journal*.

2. Jean Blackwell Hutson, "The Schomburg Center for Research in Black Culture," *Encyclopedia of Library and Information Science*, 26 (New York: Marcel Dekker, Inc., 1972). Reprinted by permission of Marcel Dekker, Inc.

3. Stanton F. Biddle, "A Partnership in Progress," *The Schomburg Center for Research in Black Culture Journal*, 1, no. 4 (Spring 1978), 2. Reprinted by permission of *The Schomburg Journal*.

4. J. Max Bond, Jr., "Schomburg's New Home," *The Schomburg Center Journal*, 2, no. 1 (Winter 1983), 1. Reprinted by permission of *The Schomburg Journal*.

SPECIAL COLLECTIONS
AT THE ATLANTA UNIVERSITY CENTER

Minnie Clayton

BACKGROUND

The brochure distributed at the dedication of the Atlanta University Center Robert W. Woodruff Library on April 23, 1982, says of the Division of Special Collection and Archives, "This major national and international collection of primary and secondary sources on the Black experience represents the 'crown jewels' of the Library's collections and consists of more than 20,000 volumes, over 1,000 non-current bound periodicals, and a large number of rare materials, artifacts and manuscripts. The archival collection includes original historical records of each of the six institutions in the Atlanta University Center."

As a single grain of sand in the sac of a pearl oyster initiates the nucleus of a pearl, one of the loveliest and most expensive of the crown jewels, a gift of "some valuable old magazines and a collection of programs, etc. [sic] with which to start an Atlanta University memorabilia,"[1] from Dr. Horace Bumstead, president of Atlanta University from 1888 to 1907, was figuratively the grain of sand that formed the very first jewel.

The "Reports of the Librarian," 1915–1916 and 1923–1924 are missing; consequently, it is impossible to document how much the symbolic pearl grew during those years. Records reveal, however, that some time during the 1924–1925 academic year, "A section of the library [had] been reserved for books about Negroes or books written by Negroes. This [proved] valuable when questions concerning

Minnie Clayton is processing archivist at the Division of Special Collections and Archives, Atlanta University Center, Robert W. Woodruff Library.

Negroes [arose]."[2] The report reveals that of 15,772 volumes that the library held on June 30, 1925, 291 were designated as "Negro" and 38 were part of the Atlanta University Collection.[3] By June 30, 1926, the Negro Collection had grown to 315 volumes and the Atlanta University Collection to 71.[4] In December 1929 Librarian F. N. Morrill, in reporting on book repairs, states, "All AU Collection and Negro Collection books have, however, been carefully repaired, and the outside of the books in both collections—numbering over 400— carefully shellacked for better preservation."[5] Even then, concern for preservation of these materials was important and it has continued to this day. The inventory of books by classes as of September 1929 showed a total of 365 volumes for the Negro Collection and 90 Atlanta University Collection volumes.[6]

No specific mention of the Negro Collection or materials about blacks in the Atlanta University Library was made in annual reports until 1936, when the purchase of the *Atlanta Independent*, covering the years from 1904 to 1928, was reported.[7] As evidenced in the 1936 to 1937 report, purchases of materials about blacks were still being made. Attention was called to the addition of "a number of rare French items pertaining to the Negro . . . ,"[8] and the "chief purchase of interest was a collection of second hand books and pamphlets relating to the Negro, the abolition movement, and American politics as affected by slavery in the period preceding the Civil War."[9] Library purchases of materials by and about "Negroes" continued in the intervening years.

THE HAROLD JACKMAN COLLECTION

An important acquisition, the Harold Jackman Collection of Contemporary Negro Life, was begun in 1942 by Harold Jackman.[10] Jackman, a black bibliophile, was a well-educated New York City public school teacher, patron of the arts, active member in many cultural and literary movements, and personal friend of that productive and prolific group of artists who flourished during the Harlem Renaissance. His outstanding collection contained books, including many inscribed and first editions, letters, manuscripts and drafts of works, poems, plays, printer's proofs, theater bills and programs, music and concert programs, newspaper and magazine reviews, advertisements

Harold Jackman was a close friend of noteworthy poet Countee Cullen and founder of the Cullen Memorial Collection at Atlanta University. (Courtesy Atlanta University Center, Robert W. Woodruff Library, Division of Special Collections and Archives, Atlanta, Georgia)

and critical notices, sheet music, and many, many Carl Van Vechten photographs. The emphasis of the collection was on contemporary life, although some older and extremely rare items were among the original gifts. Upon the death of his personal and very close friend, Countee Cullen, Mr. Jackman had this collection of Negroana named for his friend as a memorial to Cullen's great interest in the Negro and to his faith in the future of his race.[11]

From its inception, Harold Jackman, the chief sponsor, has been the greatest contributor to the Cullen Collection. In the early years, substantial contributions were made by Langston Hughes during his guest professorship at Atlanta University; Owen Dodson during his tenure at Spelman College when he was professor of speech and director of the University Players; Dorothy Peterson of Brooklyn, New York; Carl Van Vechten; and from the estate of Mr. Cullen. This outstanding collection occupied space in the facilities of the Negro Collection.[12]

The Countee Cullen Memorial Collection at Atlanta University

By Wallace Van Jackson

THE first anniversary of the death of Countee Cullen was the occasion for much interest in the books, photographs, and other materials in the collection of Negroana established in his honor at Atlanta University in Atlanta, Georgia.

The collection, officially known as the Countee Cullen Memorial Collection, founded by Harold Jackman, originated with a small gift made by an alumnus of Morehouse College in August 1942. From the beginning the chief sponsor and greatest contributor has been Mr. Harold Jackman, teacher in the public school system of New York City and friend and patron of the arts and letters. Though born in London, Mr. Jackman received his education in the public schools of New York and New York and Columbia Universities, holding an M.A. degree from the latter institution. From 1935 to 1937 he was associate editor of *Challenge*, a literary magazine edited by Dorothy West. Mr. Jackman is a life member and executive board member of the Negro Actors Guild and has been active in all artistic and literary movements which have started in Harlem.

This collection consists of theatre bills and programs, music and concert programs and bills, manuscripts, printer's proofs, newspaper and magazine reviews, books, periodicals, photographs, art programs and bills, reprints, pamphlets and broadsides, advertisements and critical notices. The emphasis is upon contemporary life although some rare older items form a part of the collection. Upon the death of the internationally known poet, Countee Cullen, Mr. Jackman had this collection of Negroana named for his friend as a memorial to Cullen's great interest in the Negro and to his faith in the future of his race.

The Countee Cullen Memorial Collection now contains more than 3,250 items, with the theatre represented by 448 pieces; music by 571 pieces, and

This collection was founded at Atlanta University by Mr. Harold Jackman in memory of his friend, the late Countee Cullen. With emphasis on contemporary life, the collection is rich in music, theatre, and periodical items

civic and political activities by 763 items. There are 450 newspaper and magazine clippings, 228 photographs, 276 periodicals and 117 pamphlets in the collection.

Among the printer's proofs are three of Cullen's books, *Ballad of the Brown Girl, Color,* and *The Lost Zoo*; and

Margaret Walker's *For My People,* the proof of Horace Mann Bond's article, "Negro Education—A Debate at the Alabama Constitutional Convention of 1901," is also included. The sixty manuscripts include Arna Bontemps' *Father of the Blues,* Gwendolyn Brooks' notebook of poems for *Street In Bronzeville, A Report of the Public School Facilities for Negroes in Atlanta,* edited by Dr. J. A. Pierce and others, organizational drafts of the program and announcement of the famous Durham, North Carolina, Conference on Race Relations," and twenty drafts by Pearl Buck, Arthur Spingarn, Carl Van Vechten, Dorothy West, Walter White, Langston Hughes, Owen Dodson, Claude McKay, and others. Among the letters is one addressed to E. I. Alexander by Captain William H. Jackman of the 48th Infantry, U.S. Army, who was stationed at Manila in the early part of the present century. The collection has the sheaf of letters of permission for the use of poems published in *Golden Slippers,* edited by Arna Bontemps. Finally, there is Clarence Cameron White's manuscript of the "Suite on Negro Folk tunes."

Photographs

The photographs form a very popular and important part of the collection. Most of them are by Carl Van Vechten and include likenesses of the outstanding Negroes of the drama, of the dance, of art, of literature, and of civic and political life who have spent time in New York City.

Music is represented by forty pieces of sheet music, the words of which were written by Countee Cullen, Langston Hughes, Claude McKay, and James Weldon Johnson, and music written by William Grant Still, Clarence Cameron White and J. Rosemond Johnson, among others. Most of this material is inscribed. The Town Hall Program

The Countee Cullen Memorial Collection was lauded in *The Crisis,* May 1947. (Courtesy *The Crisis*)

THE HENRY SLAUGHTER COLLECTION

Atlanta University's purchase of the famous Henry Slaughter Collection was the beginning of "a dream come true" for Wallace Van Jackson, university librarian. The acquisition of this enviable collection enhanced the prestige and value of the Negro Collection at Atlanta University and contributed immensely to its ever-growing holdings

84

of treasured jewels of the black experience. In his annual report Mr. Van Jackson writes:

> From the beginning of the present administration, the Librarian has believed that Atlanta University should be a great center of information on the Negro. In order to do this, it is necessary to have a large collection of materials on the Negro, properly cataloged and housed and serviced by an experienced person. We are very glad to state that the first part of this collection will be housed, together with the Harold Jackman Collection and other collections and materials already in the library, in a special room or rooms to form an important Negro collection. We hope soon to have the cataloging and processing of this material started under the supervision of a competent person. This collection will make Atlanta University the outstanding center for Negro information in the Southeast.[13]

Wallace Van Jackson's statement regarding the "famous Slaughter Collection" referred to the private library of Henry Procter Slaughter, another black bibliophile. Born in Louisville, Kentucky, young Slaughter sold newspapers at the age of six to help support his widowed mother and younger siblings. Determined to receive an education, Slaughter graduated as salutatorian of his class in Louisville and later attended Livingstone College in Salisbury, North Carolina, while working as manager-foreman of the African Methodist Episcopal Zion Church Publication House. Henry Slaughter had an insatiable desire to collect. Because of his massive library of books, broadsides, autographs, documents, and other memorabilia about blacks, "Slaughter must be included among those outstanding bibliophiles in Black studies."[14]

After moving to Washington, D.C., while employed for many years in the Government Printing Office, Slaughter spent a small fortune in his forty years of collecting. According to Bacote,[15] Slaughter owned by 1945 one of the best and largest libraries of materials by and about Negroes, and he permitted scholars recommended by the Library of Congress and Howard University to use his resources. It has been reported that in 1946, when he made the decision to sell his collection because of the safety hazards imposed by its physical size, two universities sought to purchase it. Slaughter's friendship with Dr. Rufus E. Clement, then president of Atlanta University, was said to be a factor in the sale of the collection to that university for $25,000. Also, it has been said that Mr. Slaughter believed the

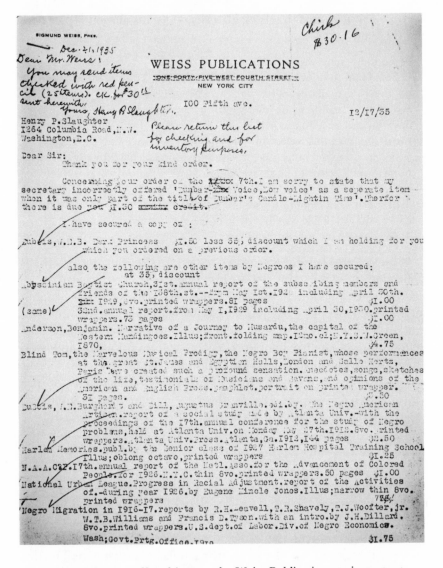

This listing of items offered in 1935 by Weiss Publications to important bibliophile Henry P. Slaughter, whose collection was acquired by the Atlanta University, reflects the role that book dealers have played in the successful collecting many of the most active collectors have been able to achieve. (Atlanta University Center, Robert W. Woodruff Library, Division of Special Collections and Archives, Atlanta, Georgia)

university would be a location where scholars would expect to find and use these literary gems and that these materials would be properly housed and cared for.[16] In his 1946–1947 annual report, Van Jackson stated that "The famous Slaughter collection is now housed in a room. . . . Miss Ellene Bentley has been employed as librarian of the Negro Collection, and is carefully but efficiently cataloging and preparing the books for use."[17] Ellene Terrell Bentley indicated in her annual report on February 4, 1947, that:

> Work on the Negro Collection of the Atlanta University Library begun *[sic]* the first of June, 1946. Mrs. Dorothy Porter, Librarian of the Moorland Foundation, Howard University Library, was here at that time, for the period of one month, to assist in organizing the Slaughter Collection. The books and pamphlets were roughly grouped on the shelves under the following headings. Slavery, Civil War, Religion, Music, Secret Societies, Art, Drama, Education, Folklore, Poetry, Fiction, Biography (White Persons), Biography (Negro Persons), The Negro Problem, Africa, Cuba, The West Indies, Haiti, and San Domingo, and South America and other countries. Since the books on Abraham Lincoln were so numerous, the majority of them were shelved in the stacks. Most of the manuscripts, photographic materials, musical compositions, newspaper clippings, and curios and museum pieces were completely organized. Procedures to be followed in organizing the collection were set up and the majority of them were set in motion. Summary reports of the number of types of materials as well as lists of some of the unique and rare volumes and other items of interest contained in the collection were submitted to the librarian.[18]

THE LINCOLN COLLECTION

In 1952 another crown jewel was donated. According to the report of Lawrence D. Reddick, university librarian, "During 1952, the library acquired a Lincoln Collection. This proved to be the outstanding feature of the year."[19] He further stated regarding the Lincoln Collection:

> The valuable Lincoln Collection that came to us through the heart-felt generosity of Mrs. Anna Chrittendon Thayer has in it some items that are not to be found in any other collection anywhere. It is important that this Lincoln Collection should be here at Atlanta University, deep

in what often seems to be "Confederate territory." In addition to its attractiveness, this permanent display should be a constant reminder that nationalism rather than sectionalism, equalitarianism rather than subordination, in any of its forms, are among the finest traditions of our University.[20]

WOODRUFF PAINTINGS

Reddick also stated in his 1952 report that "Hale Woodruff completed the installation of his paintings in the library which were six large panels depicting the history of art with emphasis on the contributions of Negro history and culture."[21] Souvenir leaflets, descriptive and other interpretive items on Woodruff's work are jewels among the files today.

THE NEGRO COLLECTION

"The Negro Collection had a dim year," reported Reddick in the 1952 report. "Successively, it lost both of its librarians; its usage fell to a low point and at the end of the year, the room was put on half-day schedule, temporarily."[22] It may have suffered in services but it held its own in terms of acquisitions. The collection received through purchase, gift and transfer, 450 items that were cataloged. Reddick mentions that the "special project" of saving the documentation of higher education among Negroes in Atlanta "moved on successfully and that Mrs. Flipper's gifts have helped immensely" on this— particularly with reference to Morris Brown and the careers of Bishops H. M. Turner and J. S. Flipper. "The outstanding deed of preservation of the year . . . was microfilming of the only file of the *Savannah Tribune* that is known to exist."[23] In 1952, the library also received Atlanta University theses, a signifiant addition, as well as other relevant acquisitions. In 1953 Reddick reported a total of 3,076 bound theses, 1,165 books classified and cataloged, in the Negro Collection, 737 in the "Old Collection" (the Atlanta University Collection), and "the big gift that came from our own School of Social Work. . .the personal library of Dr. Forrester B. Washington."[24] The acquisitions report of 1953 indicated that Dr. Washington's gift included the School of Social Work yearbooks and proceedings.[25]

"The Negro Collection is at once the favorite and the stepchild of the Library,"[26] reported Reddick, in his 1953 report, and he continued:

> It is, of course, our most valuable book collection. And yet it is located in our basement and is open only half time each day. There is just no other place to put the Negro Collection now and its limited use in part justifies its relative inaccessibility (though this is not serious) and limited hours. The other part of the explanation is that the acquisition and processing phases of this collection are so great that at present a large share of the time of the Negro Collection's librarian must be spent in gathering new things and in catching up on the accumulated pile. The numerous staff changes here since 1951 have not helped matters either. Looking ahead, we know that this department will outgrow its present quarters. As soon as we are able to keep it open full time, an organized effort will be made to publicize the treasures that we have here. It is a high compliment to these resources that a young French writer, Paul Levy, spent half a year with us writing his dissertation on American Negro Poets.[27]

The Negro Collection librarian, Marnesba D. Hill, refers to the Negro Collection and its use as a "special collection" in her 1953 report, which is the first time in the documentation of the development of the title that the term Special Collections had been used:

> The use of the Negro Collection has increased during the fall term. The librarian has frequently had to secure books for borrowers when the room is closed—these books to be used in the Reference Room and returned to the desk there. The librarian feels that this is not good practice because there is danger of books not being returned. It is felt, by the librarian, that since the Negro Collection is a special collection and a reference collection, books should be used only in the room when the librarian or student assistant can serve the borrower. The librarian also feels that interlibrary loan service of Negro Collection books should be stopped. From just a cursory examination, a number of books are missing, and it is felt that if all books are kept in the room, there is less chance of losing them.[28]

L. D. Reddick reported in 1954:

> "... the Catalog Department with part-time assistance from the

Negro Collection, processed . . .1,498 items for the Negro Collection and 2,076 from the old Atlanta University Collection which represented transfers rather than acquisitions."[29]

He further elaborated on the following details regarding donations to and use of the Negro Collection:

The Negro Collection, too, has been bursting out of its quarters. It will now have a section of stack one and will thus achieve space-room for its books and pamphlets. This department also needs additional filing cabinets and some sort of facility for its pictures and manuscripts that are steadily increasing. The estate of the late Sol C. Johnson, old militiaman and veteran publisher of the *Savannah Tribune*, gave to the library some twenty-odd pictures and other association items that help document the participation of Negro Georgians in the State Militia, 1870–1905. Our long-time friend, Harold Jackman, continues to collect for us playbills, letters, pictures and autographed copies of the works of Negro authors. The file of the Broadway and "Little Theater" plays in which Negroes have had significant roles is also steadily growing. The efforts to collect and preserve the evidences of the activities of the institutions that make up the Atlanta University Center do not show an equivalent success. Somehow we have failed to communicate sufficient enthusiasm for this endeavor to the persons that the college presidents have assigned to gathering the current programs, reports, catalogs, brochures and so forth of each campus. Despite this inertia, we are not abandoning this project.[30]

Noteworthy acquisitions to the Negro Collections were some of the manuscripts of Nancy Cunard's anthology *The Negro*, the autographed typescript of Era Bell Thompson's *Africa—Land of My Fathers* and M. Carl Holman's manuscript copies of his writings, dating back to his high school days and coming up to and including his prize-winning Yale University plays and TV dramas. The collection houses Anthony H. Richmand's manuscript of his *Color Prejudice in Britain* (Professor Richmand teaches at the University of Glasgow) and music manuscripts of Waymon A. Carver, bandmaster of Clark College. Langston Hughes gave, through Mr. Jackman, typescripts of his writings and numerous printed programs on which his name appears. Leigh Whipper's contribution included the testimonial volume entitled *To Bill Robinson, Sentiments We Cannot Forget.*

In 1955 the new chief librarian, James A. Hulbert, immediately engaged himself in reopening reading rooms and service desks for longer periods of time. The schedule of opening the Negro Collection was 9:00 A.M. to 5:00 P.M. Monday to Friday.[31]

The librarian's report for 1955 cites the significant gifts of letters of Samuel H. Archer, Sr., former president of Morehouse College, two typescripts of James Baldwin's books, and photographs and materials from Harold Jackman and Carl Van Vechten.[32] It also highlights six activities of the Negro Collection:

1. continued expansion of the card catalog to cover all types of materials;
2. reorganization of vertical files;
3. continued processing of correspondence in the Cullen Collection;
4. making theater materials more available;
5. an inventory of the collection; and
6. various exhibits.[33]

This listing may well document the beginning of a special card catalog for the Negro Collection as well as the Theater Files. It is not the first of the exhibit activities to be cited, but it is the first cited as a highlight for the Negro Collection.

A joint Library-School of Library Service exhibits committee was formed. Exhibits during the year included one for Negro History Week, an exhibit honoring President Tubman of Liberia upon his visit to the university, a number of photographs of Carl Van Vechten, and an art exhibit by the art departments of Spelman College and Clark College.[34]

In 1955, the vault was mentioned for the first time. It reveals that capacity was reached and space elsewhere should be found to store university paintings, and the suggestion was made that many materials and books might be packed to save space or moved elsewhere.[35]

The year 1956 marked the beginning of a "Library Re-Organization [when] the Negro Collection [became] a part of one of three main departments" . . . "Special Services, . . . and [was] located in the former periodical room."[36]

The Negro Collection librarian reported that gifts continued to come in. "The outstanding manuscript received was James Baldwin's *Giovanni's Room*. Dr. Hylan Lewis gave the page proofs of his book, *Blackways of Kent*. About 75 new books and pamphlets were received, 25 of which came from or through Harold Jackman."[37]

On the development of the Negro Collection, the librarian indicated in her report that:

> The most disturbing factor concerning the growth of the Collection is that the Library purchased no books during the year. All new books purchased by or about Negroes went to the General Reading Room, although order cards were sent in by the librarian of the Negro Collection. It is impossible for the room to develop if it depends only on the generosity of friends.[38]

Negro Collection librarian Marnesba Hill recommended "that money for purchasing Negro books for the Negro Collection be included in the general budget of the library."[39] This recommendation was cited in the report of the Chairman of the Library Administrative Committee[40] and the report of the Technical Services Division.[41]

It was cited in the librarian's report for 1957 under "Acquisitions" that a definite amount of $300 be allocated in the book budget for 1957–1958 so that purchases of books might be requisitioned by the librarian in the Negro Collection.[42]

Work was done in the following areas in the Negro Collection in 1957, according to the librarian's annual report:

> Inventory was taken during the year, many lost books were found, and many corrections made, manuscripts still received from Phylon and cataloging of these has continued, researchers continue to use the collection, cataloging of sheet music was begun, the Theatre Collection has been organized and cataloged for use. President Clement and Mr. Harold Jackman continue to be our best sources for theatre playbills, a special exhibit "Fifty years of the Negro in the American Theatre" was done by Mrs. Marnesba Hill and Mrs. Annabelle Jarrett, a calendar of letters in the Negro Collection has been set up so that they may be available and easily accessible to researchers, no Book Fair was held this year, the Library Staff suggests that the idea of having a Book Fair annually might be reconsidered, an Atlanta University Archive was begun in the old Negro Collection Room, it contains duplicate copies of old Atlanta University Publications, the files of the Commission on Interracial Cooperation, Council on Human Welfare, raw data on the Study of Negro Business, Old University record books, and other materials.[43]

A total of 3,526 manuscripts, 1,088 photographs, and hundreds of letters and other items[44] were reported as growth in the Negro

Collection, as reported in the librarian's annual report for 1958. The Negro Collection report is included in the Special Services section of the librarian's annual report for 1958, and the following is reported:

> Special Services include the Negro Collection, Lincoln Collection, Carnegie Prints Collection, Records Collection and Exhibits. Periodical Services were combined with these services in September, 1957. This year, under Mr. John L. Curry and with the added help of a Graduate Library Assistant, service in this area has moved forward. In addition to the regular services, 213 manuscripts were cataloged, 260 letters calendared, 273 Phylon Book Reviews and 246 play bills and programs were cataloged. As of December 1958, the Negro Collection contained, in addition to books: 1,115 Manuscripts—Slaughter Collection, 1,997 Manuscripts—Countee Cullen Collection, 1,088 Photographs, 414 Music Manuscripts, 343 Newspaper Portraits, 64 Pictures. Harold Jackman visited the Collection in April, 1958 and has continued to be the greatest and most constant donor to the Collection. Material from the Negro Collection is put on display in exhibits and is used by local students as well as by scholars from abroad.[45]

In the Library Activities section of the 1958 Librarian's Report the resignation of the Negro Collection librarian, Marnesba Hill, is indicated and she was succeeded by John L. Curry. It also states that:

> Harold Jackman, long time donor of Trevor Arnett Library and founder of the Countee Cullen Memorial Collection here, was a guest of Atlanta University in April and a special recognition was given him in the library on April 9th. About one hundred guests participated in this honor.[46]

In the Recommendations section of the Librarian's report of 1958, it is recommended that:

> The Negro Collection should be moved across the hall and a door connecting the inner office of that room and the Lincoln Collection should be provided. This would put the Special Collections together where they could be properly supervised and serviced as a unit. This would be inexpensive yet very helpful. It would provide a place for research and serious work without the noises and disturbances which tend to accompany the use of periodicals and newspapers, as is now the case. This should be accomplished before September 1, 1959.[47]

A copy of the library handout for users is included in the appendix of the 1958 Librarian's Annual Report. The segment on how to get

93

a book in Trevor Arnett Library includes a section for the Negro Collection. It reads:

> The Negro Collection is the third largest collection of materials on the Negro in the United States. It is housed in the room to your right as you enter the library. There is a catalog in the room arranged alphabetically by author, title, and subject. Fill in a call slip and present it to the person on the desk and wait to have your request filled. Materials in the Negro Collection are to be used only in the room. They do not circulate, except on special written permission of the Chief Librarian. Use these materials well in the library.[48]

This statement indicates the care and concern for the Negro Collection based on the carefully worded procedures by which the materials in the collection could be used.

The Special Services section of the 1959 report did not indicate the use of the Negro Collection but noted that gifts of 110 new titles were added to the collection along with 60 manuscripts and 24 photographs by Carl Van Vechten.[49]

The format for reporting the development of special collections changed considerably during the 1960s. Therefore, this overview will cease to document excerpts but will conclude by noting the total volumes of the Negro Collection as reported by Special Services in 1960 and the Special Services of 1961.

The librarian's report for 1960 stated that the collection included a total of 11,591 books, 1,115 manuscripts—Slaughter Collection, 2,023 manuscripts—Countee Cullen Memorial Collection, 11 vertical file cabinets (4 drawers) of which 2 include biography (clippings, articles, and photographs of individuals), 2 include Negro Colleges (information, memorabilia), 1 theater file of playbills, etc., and 6 general information on the Negro, 1,023 photographs, 343 newspapers, . . . 64 prints, and 487 music manuscripts.[50]

It was reported in 1961 that Special Services received 67 additional titles of Negro newspapers on microfilm, which strengthened the services to scholars who had indicated need of them. In 1961, the Negro Collection was being used by fewer students, but they used more material. According to the Special Services Section of Chief Librarian William Bennett's report:

> More and more we are getting requests to take materials out over night or over weekends. We have suggested that where possible, paperback

copies of titles in the Negro Collection be provided for out circulation. This would permit extended use while at the same time it would preserve those books which we fear to lose. There is not as much use made of the collection as one would expect during this period of history. The death of Harold Jackman, long time donor to the library, was felt by us. His sister contributed over 300 titles to the library from his estate. The Negro Collection continues to grow. Carl Van Vechten continues to send photographs and playbills to the Countee Cullen Collection.[51]

SPECIAL COLLECTIONS

From 1962 to the present, emphasis has continued to focus on expanding the volume of Special Collections and improving their services. This brief overview documenting their development from accessible librarians' annual reports is the initial approach to a better knowledge of the character and conditions under which these crown jewels were created.

Today, Special Collections are among the primary responsibilities of the Division of Special Collections and Archives of the Atlanta University Center Robert W. Woodruff Library. The division was established by the consolidation of Special Collections of the six institutions' libraries in the Atlanta University Center, including Atlanta University, The Interdenominational Theological Center, Clark College, Morehouse College, Morris Brown College, and Spelman College.

The purpose of the division is to preserve and service the Special Collections, including records, papers, books, artifacts, and memorabilia; to document the histories of the six institutions; and to acquire, preserve, and service other related resources to augment the institutional holdings. The uniqueness of the Special Collections required the division to have two distinct departments: the Special Collections Department for published materials including books, pamphlets, periodicals, and subject files of an ephemeral nature and the Archives Department for unpublished materials including records, manuscripts, artifacts, and memorabilia. Currently, the division is responsible for organizing the various types of materials that were brought together by the merging that began in January 1982.

Briefly, some of the major collections that were transferred to the division are as follows.

The Atlanta University Trevor Arnett Library Holdings

Three outstanding Negro Collections in this group that were to serve as a nucleus that would be augmented by others to follow are (1) the Harold Jackman Negro Collection, reported as the "most outstanding gift of the year" in 1942; (2) the "famous Slaughter Collection" purchased in 1946; and (3) the Atlanta University Archives, announced in 1957, beginning with the holdings of "Atlanta University Publications, The Commission on Interracial Cooperation (CIC) Records, Council on Human Welfare Papers, raw data on the study of Negro Businesses and early Atlanta University record books."

The Jackman Collection, now known as the Countee Cullen-Harold Jackman Memorial Collection, is on the Contemporary Negro in Literature, Art and Culture and receives regular shipments of manuscripts, books, periodicals, programs, playbills, brochures, taped performances and interviews, photographs, and announcements from Miss Ivy Jackman, Harold Jackman's sister and a member of the Harold Jackman Memorial Committee.

The Henry P. Slaughter Collection on the history of people of African descent consists of many types of materials, including correspondence, holographs, rare books, autographed books, famous signatures, periodicals, sheet music, manuscripts, prints, newspapers, monographs, and memorabilia.

The University Archives consists of administrative records of the university and its affiliations, presidential papers, faculty and staff publications, faculty and staff individual papers, unpublished manuscripts including theses and dissertations, published and unpublished papers and records of class activities, and projects and programs of the various departments and schools of the university. Because of its origin, history and southern location, the Atlanta University Archives is the recipient of many organizational archival records and papers which augment its holdings. Some of the major organizational ones include the Association of Southern Women for the Prevention of Lynching (ASWPL), 1930–1941; The Neighborhood Union (one of the earliest private social welfare agencies in Atlanta, Georgia), 1908–

1961; The Southern Conference for Human Welfare (mainly documenting the North Carolina and Washington, D.C., chapters of the conference including papers pertaining to Clark Foreman, Virginia Durr, and Mary McLeod Bethune), 1938–1948; The Southern Regional Council (publications and archives documenting functions from its inception in 1944 to the 1970s).

Some of the major individual collections donated by Atlanta University faculty, staff, alumni and friends include those of George Alexander Towns (one of the first graduates of Atlanta University), 1870–1961; C. Eric Lincoln (author and educator); Clarence A. Bacote (known as the campus historian, author, educator, Atlanta University faculty and department head); Grace Towns Hamilton (daughter of George Towns, member of the Board of Trustees of Atlanta University and Georgia State Legislature).

The Interdenominational Theological Center Library

The volume of materials that were transferred from the Interdenominational Theological Center (ITC) represents the records, papers, books, and gifts of materials that were generated from the ITC and its seven component seminaries, including Gammon (Methodist Church), Morehouse (Baptist Church), Turner (A.M.E.), Phillips (C.M.E.), Absalom Jones (Episcopal), Johnson C. Smith (Presbyterian), and Mason (Church of God in Christ) theological seminaries.

Each of these group's series of materials documents some aspect of the founding or functions of the seminaries in the ITC. The purchases and gifts are supportive type published materials for developing a collection for extensive research in the history of the black church and black theology. The oldest and largest group of materials in the ITC repository is the Gammon Theological Seminary Collection on the black experience in the Methodist Church. This collection dates back to the early nineteenth century and before with minutes, reports, official organs, news and press releases, journals, occasional papers, pamphlets, correspondence, conference memorabilia, sermons, and other primary source material that document the Methodist Church especially in the state of Georgia and bordering states.

Holdings from Clark, Morehouse, Morris Brown,
and Spelman College Libraries

The only materials that were transferred initially to the division from the libraries of Clark, Morehouse, and Morris Brown colleges were their purchased and gift Negro book collections. These collections included many of their yearbooks, histories, biographies, catalogs, campus publications, news releases, and autographed books, written by faculty, staff, alumni, and friends, and subject files of relevant clippings, biographical and historical sketches, periodical articles, photographs, and memorabilia.

Spelman College chose not to transfer its Special Collections to the division. However, many items documenting Spelman are available as part of the holdings of the other institutions in the Atlanta University Center. They are especially evident in the Atlanta University Trevor Arnett Library repository because of the Atlanta University-Morehouse-Spelman affiliation and the natural networking and sharing of materials among the librarians and the Atlanta University family.

DIVISION POLICIES AND PROCEDURES

The division has continued to provide its patrons, including students, faculty, staff, researchers, and the community at large, with resources, while active and exciting creative programs of acquisitions, processing, and servicing of materials are in progress.

Since the opening in January 1982, the staff has been involved in professional outreach activities for additional formal training and exposure while receiving on-the-job training including daily hands-on experience with the materials. Careful handling of materials takes place as staff identify, arrange, and inventory materials so that they are readily accessible for immediate retrieval. Much planning is being done for establishing permanent policies and procedures for conducting an effective operation of security, processing, and providing information for research and study.

In the meantime, relevant materials are being discovered daily and are transferred to the division for processing. The Cullen-Jackman and Slaughter Manuscripts Collections in the Archives Department

Hoyt Fuller, former director of the Institute of the Black World and editor of *Black World*. (Courtesy Atlanta University Center, Robert W. Woodruff Library, Division of Special Collections and Archives, Atlanta, Georgia)

and the materials files in the Special Collections Department serve as heterogeneous collections for depositing other donations of single items such as correspondence, holographs, poems, manuscripts, photographs, speeches, sermons, brochures, broadsides, lists, guides, charts, periodical articles, maps, and other similar items.

RECENT ACQUISITIONS

Since the merger, donations of materials have constantly been received. A description of one donation per institution follows. Atlanta University received as a gift the personal papers and library of the late Hoyt W. Fuller, which includes the largest book collection that has ever been donated to Atlanta University at one time. There are over 3,000 volumes, including books and bound periodicals, covering the black experience from Africa to America. It is exceptionally rich in black literature, history, and religion. There are also over 400

Monogram bookplate of Hoyt Fuller. (Courtesy Atlanta University Center, Robert W. Woodruff Library, Division of Special Collections and Archives, Atlanta, Georgia)

single-issue periodicals, posters, record albums, microfilm, and tapes, all in excellent physical condition.

The thirty-three linear feet of unpublished documents, including correspondence, manuscripts, photographs, and memorabilia, document Mr. Fuller's career as editor of *Negro Digest* and *Black World*, mentor to many young literary writers, and teacher, lecturer, activist, writer, and world traveler. The collection also represents his experiences as founder/publisher of *First World*. This invaluable collection was donated by Mr. Fuller's aunts, Ms. Eloise Thomas and Ms. Mattie Wiggins of College Park, Georgia. Just as the Jackman Collection was the most outstanding donation to Atlanta University in 1942 and the Slaughter Collection in 1946, so was the Fuller Collection in 1982.

The Interdenominational Theological Center (ITC) received the papers of the late Dr. Edler Garnet Hawkins, black moderator of the United Presbyterian Church in the United States of America in the 1960s. This is a very valuable collection of published and unpublished items created by Dr. Hawkins as a great preacher, theologian, and Christian leader. The collection is strong in correspondence, holographs, sermons, programs, biographical information, Presbyterian publications, and other related materials. This collection of over four cubic feet of papers was deposited by the Rev. Dr. James H. Costen, former dean of Johnson C. Smith Theological Seminary.

Clark College received a film collection on major jazz personalities and black leaders in America and a limited number in Africa. This type of collection is a "first" for the Archives Department, and the volume is over 70 cubic feet. It was donated by Mr. James Hinton, professional photographer and filmmaker of New York City. At its 1983 commencement, Morehouse College received the book collection on the black experience of one of its alumni of 1933 in celebration of his fiftieth class reunion. There are over 500 titles, strong in the area of general reference sources on the black experience, fiction, biographies, urban and rural life of black people, history, politics, and economics, deposited in the division by the alumnus himself, Dr. Edward M. Mazique of Washington, D.C.

Morris Brown College received a deposit of eleven rare books, personal copies of the late Bishop Frederick Jordan, benefactor of Morris Brown College. Three of the titles are *Quarto-Centennial of Henry McNeil Turner as Bishop in the A.M.E. Church Celebrated in St. Paul A.M.E. Church, St. Louis, Missouri, 1905; The Life, Experience, and Gospel Labors of the Rt. Richard Allen,* "Written by Himself," 1880; and *The Black Man or the Natural History of the Hametic Race,* by Rev. Joseph E. Hayne, 1894, autographed by D. J. Jordan, October 12, 1896. These books have been professionally restored for exhibition, research, and posterity and were deposited by a staff member as a transfer from Morris Brown to the division.

NOTES

1. Martha F. Emerson, "Report of Atlanta University Library," Atlanta University Library, Atlanta, Georgia (hereafter AUL), 1915. Typewritten.
2. Cora H. Adams, "Report of Librarian for 1924–25," AUL, 1925. Typewritten.
3. Ibid.
4. Cora H. Adams, "Report of the Librarian for 1925–26," AUL, 1926. Typewritten.
5. Belle C. Morrill, "Librarian's Report—Sept. 12–Dec. 18, 1929," AUL, 1929. Typewritten.
6. Ibid.
7. "Report of the Librarian," AUL, 1936. Typewritten.
8. "Report of the Librarian," AUL, 1937. Typewritten.
9. Ibid.
10. Wallace Van Jackson, "Atlanta University Library, Annual Report to the President of the University, March 1, 1943 to March 1, 1944," AUL, 1944. Typewritten.
11. Wallace Van Jackson, "The Countee Cullen Memorial Collection at Atlanta University," *The Crisis* (May 1947), 140–42.
12. Ibid.
13. Wallace Van Jackson, "Annual Report of the Librarian, 1945–46," AUL, 1946. Typewritten.
14. E. J. Josey, *Handbook of Black Librarianship* (Littleton, Colorado: Libraries Unlimited, Inc., 1977), 25–26.
15. Clarence A. Bacote, *The Story of Atlanta University: A Century of Service, 1865–1965* (Princeton: Princeton University Press, 1969), 388.
16. Ibid.

17. Wallace Van Jackson, "Atlanta University; Annual Report to the President of the University, February 1, 1946 to January 31, 1947," AUL, 1947. Typewritten.

18. Ellen Terrell Bentley, "Annual Report of Negro Collection, Feburary 4, 1947," AUL, 1947. Typewritten.

19. L. D. Reddick, "The Library in 1952," AUL, 1952. Typewritten.

20. Ibid.

21. Ibid.

22. Ibid.

23. Ibid.

24. Ibid.

25. "Librarian's Report," AUL, 1954. Typewritten.

26. Op. cit.

27. Ibid.

28. Marnesba D. Hill, "Annual Report for the Negro Collection, 1953," AUL, 1953. Typewritten.

29. L. D. Reddick, "The Library in 1954," AUL, 1954. Typewritten.

30. Ibid.

31. James A. Hulbert, "Trevor Arnett Library, Atlanta University, Annual Report of the Librarian, 1955," AUL, 1955. Typewritten.

32. Ibid.

33. Ibid.

34. Ibid.

35. Virginia Lacy Jones, "Atlanta University Trevor Arnett Library Annual Report, 1956–1957," AUL, 1957. Typewritten.

36. Marnesba D. Hill, "Negro Collection Annual Report, 1956," AUL, 1956. Typewritten.

37. Ibid.

38. Ibid.

39. Ibid.

40. Ibid.

41. Ibid.

42. "Annual Report of the Technical Services Division, January, 1956–December, 1956," AUL, 1956. Typewritten.

43. William W. Bennett, "Trevor Arnett Library, Librarian's Annual Report," AUL, 1957. Typewritten.

44. Ibid.

45. William W. Bennett, "Trevor Arnett Library, Librarian's Annual Report," AUL, 1958. Typewritten.

46. Ibid.

47. Ibid.

48. Ibid.

49. Ibid.

50. William W. Bennett, "Trevor Arnett Library, Librarian's Annual Report," AUL, 1959. Typewritten.

51. Ibid., 1960.

52. Ibid., 1961.

MOORLAND-SPINGARN

RESEARCH CENTER:

A LEGACY OF BIBLIOPHILES

Betty M. Culpepper

The mandate of the Moorland-Spingarn Research Center, founded in 1914 at Howard University, is to preserve the world-wide history of people of African descent, and to record current political, social, and cultural change affecting these people. Established seminally through the vision of Dean Kelly Miller, the generous gift of Jesse E. Moorland, and the contribution of Arthur B. Spingarn, Moorland-Spingarn today has one of the world's largest and most comprehensive collections of books, periodicals, manuscripts, sheet music, oral history interviews, sound recordings, photographs, artifacts, and memorabilia by and about black people.

BACKGROUND

Howard University was founded in 1867. Initially intended as a theological seminary to train ministers, the university was expanded later to provide for the education of doctors, lawyers, teachers, and those interested in a liberal arts education.

The university's first library consisted of books on Africa and the black experience donated by General Oliver Otis Howard, the founder for whom the institution was named. Other individuals, trustees, and faculty members contributed books dealing with the abolitionist movement and the Civil War. A most significant acquisition was that

Betty M. Culpepper is assistant chief librarian for Automatic and Technical Services, Moorland-Spingarn Research Center.

of Lewis Tappan, an abolitionist who, in 1873, deposited his considerable antislavery collection of over sixteen hundred books, pamphlets, newspapers, letters, pictures, clippings, and periodicals to the library.[1] Until approximately 1898, students and faculty operated the library on a part-time basis, opening the room for two hours several times a week. Grace Liscom Hewett-Watkins, a graduate of Simmons Library School in Boston, served as librarian from 1912 to 1916.[2]

The black history collection grew slowly during the nineteenth century but there was a steady growth of interest in studying and collecting books and documents portraying the black experience in America. Dr. Kelly Miller, a professor of mathematics and sociology (1890–1934) and dean of the College of Arts and Sciences (1907–1919), envisioned a national "Negro-Americana Museum and Library" and persuaded his friend Jesse Edward Moorland to contribute his considerable private library to the university in 1914.[3]

Jesse Moorland was born on September 10, 1863, in Coldwater, Ohio. His parents died while he was a child and his maternal grandparents reared him in New Bern, North Carolina. His grandfather often read to him from works of history and literature—John Bunyan's *Pilgrim's Progress* and Frederick Douglass's autobiography, *My Bondage and Freedom*. As a result, he read widely in literature, history, geography, and politics for the remainder of his life.

Moorland graduated from Northwestern Normal University in Ada, Ohio, and from Howard University's Theological Department in 1891. Shortly thereafter he became a Congregationalist minister and served in several churches. Later in 1891 he accepted a position as secretary of the Colored Men's Department of the Young Men's Christian Association (YMCA). Here his most noteworthy achievement was to raise more than two million dollars for YMCA buildings throughout the nation.[4]

Reverend Moorland, an alumnus and trustee, had amassed a collection of 6,000 books, pamphlets, manuscripts, portraits, and artifacts on blacks in Africa and the United States. It was hoped that Moorland's generous gift would support research and instruction in black studies as the collection was regarded as the largest and most complete one gathered by a single individual. Moorland gave his collection to Howard University "because it [was] the one place in America where the largest and best library on this subject should be constructively established. It is also the place where our young people

MY BONDAGE

AND

MY FREEDOM.

Part I.—Life as a Slave. Part II.—Life as a Freeman.

By FREDERICK DOUGLASS.

WITH

AN INTRODUCTION.

By DR. JAMES M'CUNE SMITH.

By a principle essential to christianity, a PERSON is eternally differenced from a THING; so that the idea of a HUMAN BEING, necessarily excludes the idea of PROPERTY IN THAT BEING.   COLERIDGE.

NEW YORK AND AUBURN:
MILLER, ORTON & MULLIGAN.
New York: 25 Park Row.—Auburn: 107 Genesee-st.
1855.

My Bondage and My Freedom, 1855, was the second of three autobiographies by Frederick Douglass. His writing differed from many other slave narratives of the period because it was his own work and noted for its credibility. The other autobiographies were the pioneering *Narrative of the Life of Frederick Douglass* (1845) and *Life and Times of Frederick Douglass* (1881). (Courtesy Library Division, Moorland-Spingarn Research Center, Howard University, Washington, D.C.)

This engraving of Frederick Douglass appeared as the frontispiece to *My Bondage and My Freedom*, 1855. (Courtesy Library Division, Moorland-Spingarn Research Center, Howard University, Washington, D.C.)

who have a scholarly instinct should have the privilege of a complete reference library on the subject."[5] The trustees accepted the gift collection and named it the Moorland Foundation. It was housed in the Trustee's Room of the Carnegie building and moved in 1939 to a separate room in the newly built Founders Library. The collection was the "first research library in an American university devoted exclusively to materials on the Negro."[6]

When the Moorland Foundation was established, a small staff of the Howard University Library processed the collection and made it accessible to readers. Lula V. Allan, Edith Brown, Lulu E. Connar, and Rosa C. Hershaw were among those responsible for this work.

THE PORTER LEGACY

In 1930, with the appointment of Dorothy Burnett Porter as librarian, a new era began for the Moorland Foundation. Dorothy Porter was born in Warrenton, Virginia, on May 25, 1905. She grew up in Montclair, New Jersey. A 1928 graduate of Howard University, she was the first black American woman to be awarded a master's degree in library science from Columbia University (1932). Porter credits Edward Christopher Williams, the first black American to be professionally trained in librarianship, as her mentor in black studies. She assisted him during three summers in organizing Arthur Alfonso Schomburg's Collection at the 135th Street library in Harlem.[7]

Porter took up the full-time position as curator of the Moorland Foundation in 1932 and, over the next forty-three years, devoted herself to developing its resources to serve the needs of both the university and an international community of scholars. In the 1930s, the Moorland Foundation served as a clearinghouse for materials documenting the black experience. A project of the Works Progress Administration resulted in the compilation of *A Catalogue of Books in the Moorland Foundation* and the preparation of a card file "on all publications by or about the Negro made known to the project workers by cooperating librarians in public, university and private libraries scattered throughout the country."[8] Porter recruited volunteers to index the major black periodicals—*The Crisis, The Messenger, Opportunity, The Journal of Negro Education,* and *The Journal of Negro History*—and the Howardiana Collection to preserve valuable documents of university history.

In 1946 at her behest, the university purchased the valuable 5,000 volume collection of books by black authors in the private library of Arthur B. Spingarn, a New York attorney and president of the

Dorothy Porter Wesley became librarian of the Moorland Foundation in 1930 and oversaw its growth and development for forty-three years. During her tenure many important collections were acquired and the research library became known as the Moorland-Spingarn or Negro Collection. Upon her retirement in 1973, Howard University designated a Dorothy Porter Room in the Founders Library. (Courtesy Prints and Photographs Department, Moorland-Spingarn Research Center, Howard University, Washington, D.C.)

National Association for the Advancement of Colored People. Spingarn collected rare first editions of English literature, but as he became more involved with African Americans and the problems of racism in the United States, he began to collect the literature of black authors. The Spingarn Collection was strong in its coverage of Afro-Cuban, Afro-Brazilian, and Haitian writers and contained many rare editions. Another feature of the Spingarn Collection was the large number of African writers whose works are represented as well as writers of African descent in the Caribbean, and Central and South America. The Moorland-Spingarn Collection, so named to honor the two major collectors, became "the largest and the most valuable research library in America for the study of Negro Life and History."[9]

Throughout her tenure, Dorothy Porter encouraged faculty members to make use of the collection for their own research and for class assignments. Arthur P. Davis, Harold Lewis, E. Franklin Frazier, Sterling Brown, Charles Wesley, Ralph Bunche, and Merze Tate are but a few of the major black scholars on the Howard University faculty who used the collection. Many other scholars testified to Mrs. Porter's invaluable knowledge and expertise in numerous prefaces, introductions, and acknowledgments.

During her tenure, Porter became an expert on published and unpublished materials dealing with blacks and published several books and countless articles and book reviews. In 1945, her *North American Negro Poets, a Bibliographical Checklist of Their Writings, 1760–1944* brought bibliophile Arthur Schomburg's *A Bibliographical Checklist of American Negro Poetry*, published in 1916, up to date. In 1970, *The Negro in the United States: A Selected Bibliography* was published. *Early Negro Writing, 1760–1837* was released in 1971 and in 1978, G. K. Hall published her *Afro-Braziliana: A Working Bibliography*. Upon her retirement in 1973, the university recognized Dorothy Porter's achievements with the dedication of the Dorothy Burnett Porter Room, the area that now houses the Howard University Museum.

THE MOORLAND-SPINGARN RESEARCH CENTER

In 1973, upon the recommendation of the board of trustees, the Moorland-Spingarn Collection was designated a separate administrative unit and renamed The Moorland-Spingarn Research Center (MSRC) under the directorship of Michael R. Winston, an historian and Howard University alumnus. The budget and staff were increased, and the physical facilities were enlarged and remodeled to provide additional space. The basic objectives of the collection were maintained, while the reorganization as a research center created a separate Library Division, Manuscript Division, and Support Units.

The Manuscript Division is comprised of four departments: Manuscript, Music, Oral History, and Prints and Photographs. A program of manuscript acquisition was embarked upon and the department now holds the papers of blacks in the fields of architecture, journalism, politics, social science as well as collections of organizational and institutional records. In the Manuscript Department are the papers of Alain Locke, E. Franklin Frazier, Charles C. Diggs, Paul Robeson,

Vernon Jordan, Benjamin E. Mays, George B. Murphy, Jr., Charles H. Houston, the Ancient Egyptian Arabic Order Nobles of the Mystic Shrine, the Congressional Black Caucus, and the Alpha Kappa Alpha Sorority. Primary resources total more than 400 collections spanning in excess of 6,000 linear feet.[10]

The Oral History Department is responsible for documenting, through recorded interviews, the experiences of black persons who have participated in notable historical events. The department's major resource is the Ralph J. Bunche Collection. Formerly known as the Civil Rights Documentation Project, it consists of approximately 700 interviews with a wide range of persons associated with the civil rights movement. The scope of the department has expanded beyond civil rights to include oral histories of fraternal organizations, blacks in the military, donors to the Moorland-Spingarn Research Center, and the history of Howard University. The librarian advises university and community groups to plan and conduct oral history projects.

The music librarian inventories, catalogs, and processes a large collection of sheet music and sound recordings. The largest collections in this department include those of Jesse Moorland, Arthur Spingarn, Glenn Carrington, Frank Marshall Davis, and the Washington Conservatory of Music. The bulk of the collection consists of popular music of the late nineteenth and early twentieth century with a healthy representation of spirituals, classical, and folk music. The current collection policy emphasizes the acquisition of works by black classical composers trained in the European tradition. A published guide to the nearly 4,000 compositions in the collection will be available soon, thus making the materials more accessible.

Both the Howard University community and other researchers make extensive use of the Prints and Photographs Department. Many organizations, agencies, and individuals use the collection to illustrate their projects and research. The librarian provides reference service, processes collections, prepares finding aids, solicits additional acquisitions, and mounts photographic exhibitions at the center and at other institutions as guest consultant.

The Photography Department and the Photoduplication Department ably support the center's general documentation program. In the former, photographs from the collection are copied for preservation and for use in publications, exhibitions, and films produced by scholars and researchers. In the latter, the center's large collection

The Hunted Slaves was painted in 1861 by Richard Ansdell, an associate of London's Royal Academy of Art. Inspired by Henry Wadsworth Longfellow's "The Slave in the Dismal Swamp," it reflects the mortal struggle waged by slaves in attempting to escape to freedom. This powerful piece was reproduced as an engraving in 1965 by C. G. Lewis. (Courtesy Prints and Photographs Department, Moorland-Spingarn Research Center, Howard University, Washington, D.C.)

of newspapers is microfilmed. Fragile books, periodicals, manuscripts, and other documents are photocopied for preservation. The latest technological advances in the field of photo reproduction are monitored so that the work of the department conforms to the latest professional standards.

The Library Division, the most heavily used section of the research center, is a closed stack library of some 150,000 volumes of books, newspapers, periodicals, serials, microfilms, and a vertical file of resources of ephemera, clippings, and pamphlets. In addition to the Moorland and Spingarn collections, the library of Howard University alumnus C. Glenn Carrington was obtained. Second only to the Spingarn Collection in scope, the collection contains more than 2,200 books in fifteen languages.

The Howard University Museum was proposed by Kelly Miller at the time the Jesse E. Moorland Library was donated. As early as 1868, however, the university had created a museum as part of its first library. In 1934, at the time of Miller's retirement, a committee

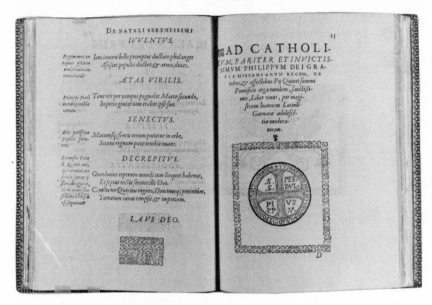

Ad Catholicum Pariter et Invictissum Philippum Dei Gratia Hispaniarum Regem, by Juan Latino, 1573, is one of the oldest and rarest books in the collections of the Moorland-Spingarn Research Center. Latino, a black slave of Granada, was one of Renaissance Spain's outstanding humanists. *Ad Catholicum* depicts King Phillip's victory over the Turks at Lepanto in 1571. (Courtesy Library Division, Moorland-Spingarn Research Center, Howard University, Washington, D.C.)

was formed to consider the creation of a museum documenting African American and African life. Dorothy Porter was among the members as were Charles H. Wesley, Rayford W. Logan, E. Franklin Frazier, Charles H. Thompson, and other university scholars. The committee's detailed report of 1938 was not acted on. The long-awaited dream of Dean Miller finally became a reality when Dr. James E. Cheek, president of Howard University, officially dedicated the Howard University Museum as part of the Moorland-Spingarn Research Center on February 12, 1979. The museum, containing sculptures, paintings, and artifacts, is primarily a teaching museum, emphasizing the visual documentation of African and African American history and culture.

The Howard University Archives, an administrative unit of the Moorland-Spingarn Research Center, collects, preserves, and organizes the university's official records, files, and documents. The archivist is responsible for the Howardiana Collection, the master's theses and doctoral dissertations housed in the Library Division. In addition, the archivist assists the university's faculties and administrative units to inventory files and records for preservation.

In his annual report for 1973–1974, Dr. Winston noted that "a research organization's strength and relative position in the world of scholarship rests upon the training, competence, and experience of its staff, no matter how rich the material resources at its disposal."[11] That is why staff training and development is stressed and staff members are encouraged to earn advanced degrees, to research topics, and to publish the results. The staff is encouraged to attend seminars, meetings, and conferences and to take an active role in various professional organizations.

Currently, the Moorland-Spingarn Research Center serves the Howard community and continues to host thousands of scholars and other visitors from many parts of the world. Dr. Michael Winston, after ten years at the helm, left the center in 1983 to assume the post of vice president for academic affairs. Mr. Clifford Muse served as acting director prior to the appointment of Dr. Thomas Cornell Battle, former curator of manuscripts, as director of the center. The Moorland-Spingarn Research Center staff looks forward to maintaining a high caliber of service to the community of scholars.

NOTES

1. Thomas Battle, "Moorland-Spingarn Research Center, Howard University," *Library Quarterly*, 58, no. 2 (April 1988), 143–63.

2. Walter Dyson, *Howard University: The Capstone of Negro Education* (Washington, D.C., The Graduate School, Howard University, 1941), 293.

3. Thomas Battle, "Moorland-Spingarn Research Center, Howard University," *Library Quarterly*, 58, no. 2 (April 1988), 144.

4. Michael R. Winston, "Jesse Edward Moorland," in Rayford W. Logan and Michael R. Winston, *Dictionary of American Negro Biography* (New York: W. W. Norton & Company, 1982), 448–52.

5. Jesse Moorland to President S. M. Newman of Howard University, December 18, 1914 in "The J. E. Moorland Foundation of the University Library," *Howard University Record* 10 (January, 1916), 5–6.

6. Michael R. Winston, "Jesse Edward Moorland," in Rayford W. Logan and Michael R. Winston, *Dictionary of American Negro Biography* (New York: W. W. Norton & Company, 1982), 451.

7. *Handbook of Black Librarianship*, comp. and ed. by E. J. Josey and Ann Allen Shockley (Littleton, Colorado: Libraries Unlimited, Inc., 1977), 30; and Dorothy B.

Porter, "Fifty Years of Collecting," in *Black Access: A Bibliography of Afro-American Bibliographies*, comp. by Richard Newman (Westport, Conn: Greenwood Press, 1984), xix.

8. "Negro Materials Catalogued by WPA Project Workers," *Hilltop* 8 (April 13, 1939), 2.

9. *The Arthur B. Spingarn Collection of Negro Authors* (Washington, D.C.: Moorland Foundation, Howard University Library, n.d. [ca. 1947]).

10. *National Inventory of Documentary Sources in the United States*, Part IV: *Academic and Research Libraries and Other Repositories* (Cambridge, Mass.: Chadwick-Healey, 1983).

11. *Annual Report, 1973–1974, Moorland-Spingarn Research Center*, Michael R. Winston, Director (Howard University, Washington, D.C., June 30, 1974), 47.

PART IV

Bibliophiles and Collectors Roundtable

BLACK GIANTS IN BINDINGS

Charles L. Blockson

The concepts of self-respect and pride are not new; they have been aged over the centuries in the highly elusive or (some say) unattainable ideal known as the brotherhood and sisterhood of humankind. Beginning in approximately 1968, however, there was a new willingness among historians to explore diverse fields in African American history, and at the same time administrators of historical repositories have shown more care in locating and publicizing relevant collections and documents. Even though a more open climate has recently developed with respect to African American history, one should realize it comes only after centuries of agitation primarily by blacks and sympathetic whites over the accuracy of America's chronicles.

"Remove as far as practical from all observation and association, every influence which tends to weaken your self respect," said Thomas Morris Chester, the outspoken black activist of the Civil War era, on December 9, 1862, when he addressed the Philadelphia Library Company during its twenty-ninth anniversary. Chester emphasized that literary contributions played a key role in the development of "self-respect and pride of race." He poignantly underscored "the superiority which the race has displayed under the most humiliating and disheartening circumstances," and he stressed that "the concealed facts of the past should be reproduced to vindicate our susceptibility to a high order of excellence." The Philadelphia Library Company was the first successful literary institution of its kind in the nation. Its library, containing more than 600 books, pamphlets, and periodicals, was housed in the basement of St. Thomas African Episcopal Church.

Charles Blockson is curator of the Charles L. Blockson Collection at Temple University.

I consider book collecting one aid in the development of pride and self-respect; and I consider book collecting one aid to understanding, which is after all a prerequisite to self-respect.

THE ECONOMICAL ASPECT

Yes, a mystery ignited my love for book collecting, and since it happened so long ago, I am happy to say that it had nothing to do with what I call the current crash program to purchase black literature; in fact, the sudden spotlight now blazing on black literature has been a deterrent to my collection. Although I am glad that black writers, past and present, are finally gaining recognition long denied them, I do sometimes long for the days not long past when I would ask a bookseller for black literature, and he would throw at me whatever items he had—just to rid himself of them. I was eager enough to catch any book thrown at me in those days. I still am.

Booksellers are no longer apt to throw such items at me, and I have mixed emotions regarding the phenomenon. Booksellers today cling to black literature much the same way Americans once clung to gilt-edged stocks, before the gilt wore away from the market.

During the past twenty years, black literature, almost to the book, has increased enormously in value. I know because I have lived through it. Black literature (to remain for a moment in the economic world) will continue to increase in value, and I base my theory on the theory of numbers—supply and demand.

First, more and more blacks are being born; second, large numbers of blacks are attending college; third, increasing numbers of blacks are attaining positions in which book collecting becomes attractive. Generations of blacks struggled to survive—some still do; however, more and more are finding enough leisure time to indulge themselves with a hobby. They are finding enough time to become interested in their heritage, their culture; they are becoming aware of it.

Contemporary books by blacks are being published in large numbers, but print runs of blacks' works of a century ago or even thirty years ago were small. The economics of the situation made large print runs unwise. Most blacks of those eras were illiterate or semiliterate; hence, black literature appealed only to those blacks who could and wished to read and whites who were interested in this culture in their midst. Supply and demand again. Today, with more blacks becoming collectors and every college and university bidding on whatever is left to collect, a ten cent book of twenty years ago has become a ten dollar book of today.

MOTIVATION FOR COLLECTING

What makes a collector collect? The hoarding instinct? A fascination and curiosity about the past? The desire for immortality? People have different motives. For me books are friends. They are people.

People are crammed between the walnut standards lining my den. Inside the books that fill my shelves are legions of personalities, witnesses to the prowess of the giants among black men and women, varied in color, stance, and nation, who have paraded before the grandstands of time.

The day came for me during my childhood when I realized the need to discover the history that lay behind the rubbled black civilization. Eventually, I began to wonder about my roots in time as well. There came a day in the fourth grade when the class was studying history. Our teacher was one of those well-programmed products of the normal school tradition, armed with the daily lesson plan from which we seldom varied. Our subject on this morning was Benjamin Franklin's inventions and almanacs, and as I listened, it occurred to me that all the references were pronounced tributes to the accomplishments of white Americans. Aside from the most obvious credits to Booker T. Washington and George Washington Carver, it was as if black people had not participated in history other than as a passive revolving point for the great American Civil War. When my turn came to pose my question for the day I asked very simply, "Do Negroes have a history?"

"No," she assured me without a hint of questioning. "Negroes have no history. They are meant only to serve white people."

For the first few moments I sat stunned, dreadfully aware that the faces surrounding me were white. I had never before been confronted with the seeming inferiority conferred by the color of my skin. In that most humiliating moment, I felt trapped between the dual images of the integrity I wanted to exercise and the subservience she associated with me. It would have been impossible to try to reason such a brutal answer and so I sat dumb, sensing more than knowing that her assessment must be inaccurate.

Out of the confusion of the moment grew a sense of anger so great that I set about deliberately seeking information about my background, the history of my people. Even before I knew it, I became a collector. Shortly after this incident I began to frequent rummage sales, church bazaars, thrift shop outlets, and used-book stalls that sold what I sought at prices I could afford. When remainder houses ran special clearance sales through these outlets, I took advantage of my proximity to pick up works that nobody thought mattered then. It was during this time that I became familiar with the local book-hunting grounds to which I owe the acquisition of some notable parts of my collection today. Best of all, I was becoming a master of the ruse, carefully dressing in a casual manner so as to appear inconspicuous as a collector. I had learned early that prices vary on books according to the amount of interest expressed in them, and so as I approached my high school years, I was already a wary shopper, searching attentively and talking very little.

I remember one day I found a book written by Dr. Carter G. Woodson, the twentieth-century historian who founded Negro History Week. More than anything, his stature and writings disproved my teacher's contention that blacks had no higher purpose than servitude.

With some amazement I learned that blacks had succeeded well in countries other than my own. According to the rules established on race, such greats as Aesop, Alexandre Dumas, and Alexander Puskin were black by ancestry. I found, too, that American black accomplishments extended beyond the literary world to include the likes of Marian Anderson, George Washington Carver, Dr. Ralph Bunche, and no less than my personal hero, Paul Robeson.

Today I have over 10,000 books, broadsides, prints, pamphlets, and sheet music in my collection, all of which speak to the breadth of the black experience. They are written in many languages, including Hebrew, French, Spanish, Dutch, Arabic, Amharic, and various African dialects. I might also add that I collect the works of whites with positive images of blacks; and I collect the writings of those who hated our race because their works, too, are an important part of black culture.

PERSONALITIES

The years have not been without their disappointment—I mean in the way of book collecting. For instance, in 1969, when I went to New York City's Metropolitan Museum to browse, I became sidetracked, as is my wont, to the University Book Store, owned by Walter Goldwater, a dealer who has specialized in black literature for more than thirty years. He is an interesting conversationalist, having known all the famous black book collectors. I purchased a few books from him that day. One was *The Fugitive Blacksmith, Or Events in the History of James W. C. Pennington*, a slave narrative, written in 1850 and published in London. Pennington had been a slave in Maryland, escaped, and later became an outstanding abolitionist.

Later that day I boarded the train to Philadelphia. On the way I began to read the Pennington book, became engrossed in it in fact. When the train reached Philadelphia I also forgot to note where I was. When I did, I set the Pennington book on my seat in order to have both hands to remove my other books from where I had placed them on the overhead. I then promptly left the train, leaving James W. C. Pennington on my seat. The book has been haunting me ever since; I hope that whoever found it is a collector. I have seen only two other copies of the book—at The Library Company and at Howard University. I had purchased my copy for four dollars. I have seen it cataloged recently at forty-five dollars.

On another occasion, I visited Sam Kleinman's Schuylkill Book Store in Philadelphia. What Sam does not know about books is unknown, and he is quite willing to share his vast amount of booklore. A trip to his store is worth the time just to listen. What I heard that day, however, was both enlightening and sad. I heard about the sale of Paul Robeson's books—one month after the event. I went to the Argosy Book Store in New York, the sellers of the Robeson material, only to discover that almost everything was already sold. I did manage to buy four items signed by Robeson, but, since Robeson had always been my hero, I was disappointed that I missed most of the sale.

Another bookdealer who influenced me was the late Lewis Michaux who entered my life during my early years of collecting. Mr. Michaux owned the National Memorial Bookstore, which was once located on 125th Street and Seventh Avenue in Harlem, New York. This spry

In Chesterfield County Court Clerk's Office, *Sept 14th* 18*58*

Richard Tho' Cogbill a free *man* of color, who has been heretofore registered in the said office, this day delivered up to me *his* former certificate of registration, and applied for a renewal of the same, which is granted *him* ; and *he* is now of the following description, to wit: age **2 0 —** years, color *mulatto* , stature *five* feet **4 3/4 Inches**, *Has a scar on the right temple & was born free in Chesterfield County*

No. *3 2 / 7*

In Testimony Whereof, I have hereunto set my hand and affixed the Seal of the said County Court, this *14th* day of *September* A. D., one thousand, eight hundred and *fifty eight* and in the *83rd* year of our Independence.

Silas Cheatham Co

Former No. *1767*, Date *13 Feb 1849*

A certificate of freedom for Richard Thomas Cogbill, extending his registration and noting that he was born free in Chesterfield County, Virginia, ca. 1838. (Courtesy Manuscripts Department, Moorland-Spingarn Research Center, Howard University, Washington, D.C.)

and witty man, with his discerning sense of honesty, guided me in selecting hundreds of books during his lifetime. I knew that "the professor," as he loved to be called, was respected by just about everyone associated with the Harlem community. The sort of people who were likely to visit his store were such authors as James Baldwin, Alice Childress, Langston Hughes, John O. Killens, and John Henrik Clarke, to name a few. Mr. Michaux once introduced me to Malcolm X, one of our leading orators.

In 1969, after the *Christian Science Monitor* wrote a story about my collection, Mr. Michaux sent me a letter that reveals the mirthful warmth beneath the cautious surface of his public attitude.[1] The letter is one of those treasured items that I have received:

> I . . . noted that very fine headline about you and your collection. Although your collection may have started as a hobby, it has become

This depicts an heinous crime that was sometimes perpetrated against free blacks, even in the nation's capital. Families were torn apart, parents resisted desperately, and serious injury and death were not uncommon. (Courtesy Prints and Photographs Department, Moorland-Spingarn Research Center, Howard University, Washington, D.C.)

an asset to you and an incentive for all the young Blocksons that will come after you.

I show this article to all the book collectors and they want to know from whence (sic) you come. I tell them you come from the grass roots and your vast collection represents the branches of these roots.[2]

What Mr. Michaux gave me was more than just simple encouragement. His contact with an era that preceded my own, having been conversant with landmark writers before I was born, provided me with personal insight and direction as to the course of literature during and after the Harlem Renaissance, and it is to him that I owe so much credit for the progress of my collection until I began to meet other collectors.

Dr. Dorothy Porter Wesley also had a profound influence upon my development as a collector. We have a warm and friendly relationship. For the past forty years, collectors of African American history and literature have received a significant portion of their knowledge from her pioneering work in preserving black writings. The bibliographies of Dr. Porter Wesley are indispensable.

I am also grateful to Dr. Jean Blackwell Hutson, Mr. Ernest Kaiser,

Dr. Jessie Carney Smith, Dr. Michael Winston, and Ms. Ann Allen Shockley for their encouragement.

PRACTICES

Hunting for books sometimes uncovers thrilling surprises. For example, once in an obscure rural area in the Pennsylvania Dutch country not far from my home, I went into a musty old store similar to the ones to which sharecroppers used to go. Herbs hung from the ceiling and big jars of rock candy were on the shelves. There I found a cardboard box full of books. As I dug through the books, I came upon a real treasure—a rare copy of Prince Saunders's *Haitian Papers*. What a find! The shopowner sold it to me for five dollars. He failed to recognize the value of books relating to black history. Valuable rewards await the patient collector in out-of-the-way second-hand bookstores.

Among the unique items I have included in my collection are the contemptible books, broadsides, and pamphlets. My earliest broadsides date back to the 1800s. One is a satire pertaining to blacks imitating whites. This series was commonly called "Life in Philadelphia." In the terminology of the book trade they are considered "damn rare." Although offensive and ludicrous, these documents are nevertheless important to collect because they portray a part of our cultural heritage. A black Americana auction held in Timonium, Maryland, drew nearly 300 buyers, according to Ronald Rooks, a Baltimore dealer. Although the major portion of the auction represented contemptible items, nevertheless, several important books were auctioned off.

I have made it a practice over many years of collecting to obtain children's books whenever possible. I can still recall Dr. Arthur Huff Fauset's book *For Freedom* that told of the deeds of outstanding black men and women. Presently, there are a number of outstanding black writers of children's literature. Four of them are Alice Childress, Virginia Hamilton, Lucille Clifton, and Kristen Hunter Lattany. I would strongly encourage novice collectors to include children's books among their holdings. But remember, whatever you buy and wherever you buy it, be sure to record the date, the dealer's name, and the price of the book. This knowledge will add to the historic and aesthetic value of the book.

Every collector has a few books that he or she values, as much for their associations as for their textual contents. For example, in my collection I have the first edition of Phillis Wheatley's *Poems of Various Subjects, Religious and Moral* (1773). Although her poetic style is archaic by today's standards, the book is a cornerstone of any collection of African American history and literature. I appreciate the book because it is autographed by her.

I have made it a practice to attain copies of books signed by their authors whenever possible. I would encourage other collectors to do so as well. If possible, collect originial manuscripts, if they are available. Author's galleys are also very valuable.

I have discovered through my collecting that books can vary greatly in price. Some dealers take advantage of the collector because black history and literature books are now highly sought after. Novice collectors should beware of such opportunists. Therefore, black scholars and collectors must develop guidelines for pricing rare documents. Occasionally, I visit auction houses in pursuit of books. Whenever possible, I visit the auction house before to look over the books being auctioned to decide on the price I should offer for an item.

Perhaps the most famous auction house connected with the sale of African American books was the Parke-Bernet auction house in New York City. Several years ago this establishment auctioned off the remainder of Arthur Spingarn's collection. Although I did not attend the auction, I was amazed when I read the price list of the auction later. Books were selling in a range from twenty-five dollars a lot, which is five to eight books, all the way up to the sale of Frank Webb's "damn rare" book, *The Garies and Their Friends*, which sold for $360.00

I have made many trans-Atlantic phone calls in purchasing books. It is imperative that modern collectors visit the bookstores abroad as well as in the United States in order to identify and collect rare books and documents. Speaking of overseas travel, Clarence L. Holte, my bibliophile friend, set a precedent in the sale of his private collection to Ahmadu Bello University for nearly a half million dollars. This price set a high standard of value on African American books and served as a guide in negotiating the establishment of my collection,

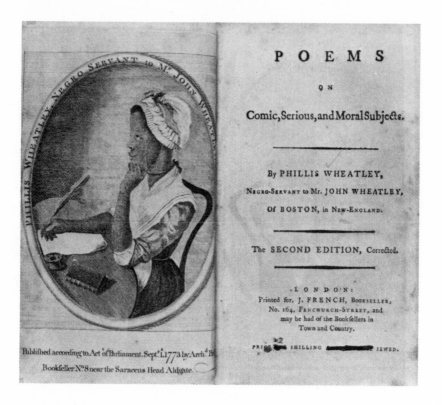

Phillis Wheatley (1753?–1784) was purchased off a slave ship in 1761 by Boston merchant tailor John Wheatley and educated in his home. She published her first poem in 1770. Wheatley's only book was planned during a trip to London in 1773 and published following her return to America. *Poems on Various Subjects, Religious and Moral* contained thirty-eight poems. (Courtesy Library Division, Moorland-Spingarn Research Center, Howard University, Washington, D.C.)

which is now housed at Temple University in Philadelphia, Pennsylvania.

Four of the finest collections of black history compiled during this century belonged to the following men: Arthur A. Schomburg, Arthur Spingarn, Henry P. Slaughter, and Clarence L. Holte. Other early collectors were such men and women as Richard Moore, Charles Martin, Leon Gardiner, Daniel Murray, William C. Bolivar, Professor William S. Scarborough, Robert Adger, William Dorsey, David Ruggles, Ella Smith Elbert, Pauline Young, and M. A. "Spike" Harris.

One of the advantages these early collectors enjoyed was the supply of important books on the market. However, their great disadvantage was that they had few bibliographical guides to assist them in identifying the race of the authors. The collector and would-be collector should study the bibliographies pertaining to the subject. They are the tools of the trade. The collector must also devour catalogs issued by bookdealers both past and present, especially those published by Charles Heartman, Walter Goldwater, and Phillip McBlain. Vernon Loggins's *The Negro Author* is another useful book for identifying the works of black authors.

Beware of attempting to cover every area of this absorbing pursuit. Because of the current inflation, the amateur collector should specialize in one or two areas. It is still possible to build a satisfying collection as I did at a modest cost. If the book is rare, purchase it in any condition until you can locate a better copy. For example, Henry Gates, Jr., distinguished author and scholar, purchased a copy of *Our Nig*, the neglected novel that altered the history of black literature, for fifty dollars from William French of the University Place Bookshop in New York City. Although this copy lacked several pages, it had historical importance. Gates later purchased a complete copy from bookseller Howard Mott.

Many rare and unusual items are included in my collection. Special strengths within the collection are the following: John Brown, Paul Robeson, blacks in Pennsylvania, the Underground Railroad, slave narratives, the Caribbean influence, biographies, novels, art, music, church histories, sports, and books pertaining to black women. The span of other items represents African heritage and the black experience in America and extends beyond the special strengths of the collection. I am proud of our past and our place in the cultural history of the world.

CONCLUSION

One way of maintaining that history is through the establishment of societies similar to those literary societies that were formed by our forefathers and mothers during the nineteenth century. Some of the great American book clubs—the Grolier Club of New York, the Philobbilon Club of Philadelphia, the Club of Odd Volumes of Boston, and the Rowfant Club of Cleveland were formed as a pleasant oasis for book lovers. The formation of clubs of this type within the black community would not only provide an important network among bibliophiles but would also contribute to the understanding of the black experience and would make the preservation of our heritage more meaningful to the general public.

NOTES

1. See Margaret Powell, "An Avid Collector of Afro-American History," *The Christian Science Monitor*, April 29, 1969.

2. Michaux to Charles Blockson, May 15, 1969, in the author's possession. Reprinted by permission of Mrs. Lewis H. Michaux.

THE ROMANCE
OF INCIDENTAL ADVENTURES
IN COLLECTING BOOKS

Clarence Holte

The idea of bringing together Afro-American bibliophiles is timely, constructive, and responsive to observations expressed in an essay by Dr. Hanes Walton, Jr., professor of political science at Savannah State College. It is entitled "The Literary Works of a Black Bibliophile," published in the December 1977 issue of *The Western Journal of Black Studies*, Washington State University, and in the July-October 1978 issue of *The Black Educational Review*, published in Jacksonville, Florida. "Black bibliophiles," declares Dr. Walton, "are rarely known, rarely seen, rarely written about and, for the most part, they rarely exist."

The fact that black bibliophiles are few in number intensifies our zeal in picking up where our revered pioneer bibliophiles left off as the reaper took his toll. The contributions of Robert Adger, Daniel Murray, Jesse Moorland, Arthur Schomburg, and Henry Slaughter are monumental and inspire us as new-day disciples, who are dedicated to combat the age-old debilitating doctrine of racism as advanced by the French diplomat and Orientalist Count Arthur J. de Gobineau and others of his conviction. *The Inequality of Human Races* by de Gobineau, written in 1853, was translated and published in English in 1916. This pseudoscientific doctrine is still alive and incubating, as seen from the duplicity and contradictions over human and civil rights and the resurgence of the Ku Klux Klan.

Clarence Holte is a well-known bibliophile who speaks and writes frequently on the subject.

We cannot afford to relent in our efforts to collect and preserve the scholarly works that categorically refute Count de Gobineau and his ilk. We have to ensure that our future generations will have exposure to books such as *The Ruins*, by Count Constantin Volney, a French historian, first published in 1791 and later translated into several English editions; *African Glory: The Story of Vanished Negro Civilization*, by J. C. deGraft-Johnson, a Ghanaian scholar, first published in 1954; *The Destruction of Black Civilization: Great Issues of a Race from 4500 B.C. to 2000 A.D.*, by Chancellor Williams, retired Howard University professor of history, first published in 1971; *The African Origin of Civilization: Myth or Reality*, written by Cheikh Anta Diop, a Senegalese scholar, first published in 1955 and translated into English in 1974; and *Africa Counts*, by Claudia Zaslausky, published in 1973. There are, of course, the works of Woodson, Du Bois, and a number of other scholars, whose works in and out-of-print must be preserved. Availability of these books is the only way future generations, at an early age, may learn what the history and culture of black people are all about and acquire the pride, self-esteem, and social control that this knowledge engenders.

GENESIS OF A BIBLIOPHILE

My late orientation to books about our heritage began during my freshman year at Lincoln University in Pennsylvania. The knowledge was sought primarily to overcome embarrassment, as well as to improve my intellect, not knowing that the subject would prove to be extensive and captivating.

In several conversations with African students there were instances in which I was expected to comment about the life and institutions of African Americans. The inability to comply adequately was embarrassing, and this reflection on my intelligence prompted me to read, as an extracurricular activity, *The Negro in Our History*, by Carter G. Woodson, and *The Souls of Black Folk*, by W. E. B. Du Bois. The instances of embarrassment proved to be a blessing in disguise in that these books were unexpectedly enlightening and sowed within me an abiding devotion to the subject of black life and culture.

After leaving Lincoln to make a place for myself in the world, I was enlivened by purchasing and reading as many books on the subject as my resources and time permitted. My books formed a "reading collection." The number grew steadily and, in due course, purchases included books to use principally for reference purposes. This process is the evolution of my becoming a devout bibliophile.

During my early days of collecting, most of the out-of-print books, now considered rare, were still available at modest prices except in New York City. There, prices were generally influenced by an astute dealer who was able to specialize in the field by having a network of out-of-town dealers supply him with books on the subject. Hence, his prices had to reflect profit for the operation.

While my collection was growing, I had the good fortune to assume a staff position with an international advertising agency. Travel was required, and this enabled me to establish relationships with dealers in a number of key cities, with whom regular contact was maintained by telephone. This development proved bountiful in obtaining many sought-after books and without premium cost. My collecting Afro-Americana, in particular, was now in high gear.

As confidant to Nnamdi Azikiwe of Nigeria, Kwame Nkrumah of Ghana, Sylvanus Olympio of Togo (each became president of his country), and several other West African dignitaries on their visits to this country in the late 1940s and during the 1950s, I found my interest in Africans and the continent expanding. I discovered, however, that the best out-of-print books about Africa were most likely to be found in England. In time, travel on several occasions made it convenient for me to spend a few days in antiquarian shops in London, Oxford, and Cambridge. The books I acquired at these shops were exceptional, and these sources were added to my network.

These purchases, together with those subsequently obtained in Nigeria, gave the collecting a rich dimension. Dealers with roadside stalls in Lagos and Ibadan, specializing in pamphlet material of various kinds, came to know me and learned of my interest. Sometimes they would obtain valuable out-of-print books and hold them for me.

In compiling a body of West African writings in English, I initially acquired works produced in the eighteenth and nineteenth centuries. These include the following: *Letters of the Late Ignatius Sancho* (two volumes, London, 1783); *Thoughts and Sentiments on the Evil and Wicked Traffic of the Human Species*, by Ottobah Cugoano (London, 1787); *Narrative of the Life of Olaudah Equiano or Gustavus Vassa, the African* (two volumes, London, 1789); *The Journals of the Rev. James Frederick*

131

Schon and Mr. Samuel Crowther (London, 1842); *Vocabulary of the Yoruba Language—Part I, English and Yoruba—Part II, Yoruba and English,* by Samuel Crowther, compiler (London, 1849); *A Vocabulary of the Yoruba Language,* by Rev. Samuel Crowther (London, 1852); *The History of Sierra Leone,* by A. B. C. Sibthorpe (London, 1868); *History of the Gold Coast and Asante Based on Traditions and Historical Facts, Comprising a Period of More than Three Centuries from about 1500 to 1860,* by Rev. Carl Christian Reindorf (Basel [Switzerland], 1895); and *Fanti Customary Laws: A Brief Introduction to the Principles of the Native Laws and Customs of Fanti and Akan Sections of the Gold Coast,* by John M. Sarbah (London, 1897).

For sequence to these pioneer writings, I also acquired works published during the first half of the twentieth century. The authors include J. E. Casely Hayford and Africanus B. Horton, M.D., of the Gold Coast; Chief I. B. Akinyele, Adebesin Folarin, Jacob Egharevba, Ajayi Kolawole Ajisafe, and Rev. Samuel Johnson of Nigeria. *The History of Lagos,* by John B. Losi (Lagos, 1914), was in my collection but not his *History of Abeokuta* (Bosere [Nigeria], 1924).

The interesting history of this former autonomous state surrounded and protected by huge rocks, and about three hours by road from Lagos, influenced me to visit the city to search for this book by Losi. "Mammy wagons" were the convenient and adventurous means of transportation. These wagons are wide-bodied trucks with bench seating and a railed top for carrying anything that could be accommodated. A young Yoruba man who had attended school in Abeokuta was engaged to accompany me. He took me first to the school, and the friendly principal referred me to an associate he hoped could be helpful. After a series of referrals, I found the book. It was in fairly sound condition, dirty, and the back cover perforated with ant holes. Finding it was exhilarating, fulfilling, and compensation for the anxiety and efforts I expended.

A number of other exciting finds could be noted, for the romance of incidental or spinoff adventures was sometimes ennobling, spiritually, emotionally, or intellectually elevating. These benefits heightened the joy of collecting.

Knowledge culled from reading books in my collecting activities made me wish to see other persons indoctrinated to black history, for the need was urgent. In this connection, I thought that it might be possible to interest some client of the advertising agency, having

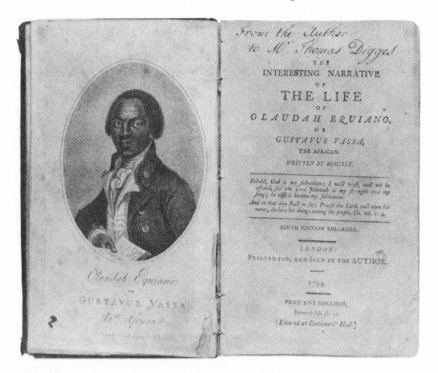

The only known autographed copy of the autobiography of Gustavus Vassa, known as Olaudah Equiano. Published in numerous editions, this account of Vassa's early life, enslavement, and subsequent freedom contributed to the abolition of the British slave trade. (Courtesy Library Division, Moorland-Spingarn Research Center, Howard University, Washington, D.C.)

a well-known and highly regarded product or service, to use a praiseworthy aspect of black history and culture as a theme for a public service campaign. Such a promotion had never been done before on a national basis.

The National Distillers Products Company wanted a proposal for its Old Taylor brand of distilled spirits, and the "Ingenious Americans" series was conceived. This series revolved around black scientists and inventors whose contributions were invaluable in the establishment and development of America. After eighteen months of wrangling, the proposal got off the back burner and in 1966 the campaign began in black newspapers and *Ebony* magazine.

The "Ingenious Americans" series was highly praised from the start. In order to fulfill the demand for tear sheets, two sets of booklets reproducing them were printed. Tens of thousands were distributed through retail stores and thousands more were used in filling mail requests. The company was so pleased with this campaign, it had small busts molded of the personalities, with the explanatory copy pasted on the bottom of the bust. These figures, made of a sand composition, were offered at the nominal cost of production, five dollars. The demand for them was very brisk, and a second shop was enlarged to produce them. The cost was higher, but it was absorbed by the company.

The series came to the attention of The Traveller's Times in New York City, a company contracted to produce and display car-cards in buses and subways in fifteen major cities and Fitchburg, Massachusetts, with twelve buses—exposure to a general audience, reportedly, of twelve million riders daily. In 1967 the company arbitrarily used the series as a public service feature. This development, to me, was earthshaking—the culmination of a dream, notwithstanding some contrary views. The campaign ran some six years and received numerous citations and awards. The resounding success paved the way for emulation by other national advertisers.

Seeing the success of the series and the present number of well-produced campaigns gives me joy for initiating a way to dramatize aspects of black history with utmost dignity and to disseminate it to the masses in the national black community. There is no doubt that these campaigns have, and are, motivating the interest of more people in the subject than could be done otherwise.

In the 1960s, there was an escalating demand by schools and libraries for out-of-print books of every genre about black people, and companies in the reprint business sought advice from able consultants regarding selection of books and where they could be obtained. Johnson Reprint Corporation in New York City, the largest international company, commissioned me, on a royalty basis and as editor, to select one hundred nonfiction books from my collection for reprinting and to write synopses of them. The series was entitled "The Basic Afro-American Reprint Library," with credit to the Clarence L. Holte Collection.

After federal funds were cut drastically for schools and libraries (the primary market for reprints), the reprint business suffered a decline and the series was limited to fifty-two titles, which totalled

27,000 books. Nevertheless, the series was gratifying because it exposed more insightful books to people concerned about black history.

Another opportunity for the collection to be of service came from L. H. Stanton, publisher of *National Scene*, a monthly magazine supplement that appears in some forty black-oriented newspapers. Stanton wanted essays based on material from my collection. I accepted the invitation and I wrote twenty-three essays over a three-year period. Mail responses indicated that the essays were obviously well received, particularly the "Presence of Blacks in Pre-Revolutionary Russia and Its Impact on Culture," in the October-November 1974 issue, and reprinted in the April 1981 issue of the *Journal of African Civilization*, and the "Unheralded Realities of North America, 1619–1776," in the Bicentennial Issue, January–February 1976.

Dr. Walton, in his essay referred to previously, comments on the body of these essays in stating that Holte had "gone beyond mere vivid imagination and creativity" and had "begun to develop something new in Black journalism . . . bringing to the masses a specialized area of Black history . . . as well as the role of Blacks throughout the world."

As a result of the appeal of these essays, I received commissions in 1979 and 1980 to write in-depth essays for syndication to some eighty black-oriented newspapers for their Black History Month issues. The first of these essays was entitled "Black Pioneers in Business: A Brief Interpretative History, 1650–1900"; the second was "The Early Black Christian Church, Its Forerunners, 3100 B.C.–1900 A.D.," and the third was "Statistics: A Brief Interpretative History."

The brochures used for selling space to national advertisers in these issues of the newspapers highlighted the essays as the work of the creator of the "Ingenious Americans" series. This factor was a salient selling point since I was a person known and respected by the advertising fraternity. This was also the first time that the newspapers had gotten in-depth essays on the two subjects. They were run in single issues or as a two-part series in some newspapers; in others, they were condensed for lack of space. Whichever the case, the mail, reportedly, was heavy.

My most pleasurable adventure as a bibliophile was the use of my collection of some 8,000 books as a major exhibit at the Second World Black and African Festival of Arts and Culture (FESTAC), sponsored by fifty-five African countries, and held in Lagos and Kaduna, Nigeria, January–February, 1977. The invitation covered every conceivable expense: stipends for me, engaged as curator, for my wife, and for two accompanying assistants; the cost for the best living accommodations; and a car and driver.

The observation that pleased me most was the obvious enhancement of pride the collection generated. This was evidenced by statements and expressions on the faces of the thousands of viewers who could hardly conceive of the fact that this massive number of books had been written about black people. Some of them were so entranced that they stood in one place for more than an hour gazing at the collection. And not a book was lost.

While the collection was being unpacked, the librarian at Ahmadu Bello University in Zaria, Nigeria, came by. Impressed by the quality of the collection, he asked if it could be purchased. My reply was vague since the collection was not brought to the festival for that purpose. He described the facilities of the new, modern $3 million university library, its dire need for the collection, and the utility it would have in facilitating African scholarship. There was no question about the merits of his thesis. It satisfied my ultimate objective for acquisition of the collection by a university with these facilities. A price was agreed upon without tugging, and a contract was signed after the librarian checked about the availability of funds.

In 1981, the university invited me to the dedication of the Clarence L. Holte Room—the repository of the collection. The occasion was a highlight in my life. While I was in Zaria, Nigeria, to attend the dedication ceremony, I visited "Old Zaria"—the original village before a town and then a city were built around it. Its recorded history extends from about 900 A.D. Amina, the second queen of the two who appear in Hausa history, succeeded to the throne of Zaria in 1576, after forty-one years of proving her prowess in battles. She built a high mud wall extending more than 100 miles around and beyond the village of mud houses to protect it and to effect control over the occupants. She is said to have founded the most powerful state of Central Sudan, conquering every village within her reach and building mud walls around them. She traveled extensively and, according to legend, chose a spouse at each village where she stopped, beheading him when she left. Amina died in 1610. Walled cities are her enduring legacy.

Going to "Old Zaria" was being in the midst of an ancient but living civilization. The wall now only surrounds the village itself. The numerous houses are still constructed of mud, clean and widely spaced as family compounds; some are painted and have two or three stories, with outside wooden ladders. Men, observed dying cloth in their traditional way, seemed to be pursuing a major occupation. It was my privilege to have an audience with the Emir, a college-trained man seemingly between thirty and forty years old. He apparently took great pride in administering this historic village. This incidental adventure brought the old world into sharper focus and increased my regard for the power of traditions and the fortitude of those who abide by them.

Last, but not least, is the honor accorded me in 1977 by The Twenty-First Century Foundation in New York City, which named a biennial international literary prize after me that recognizes a significant contribution by a living writer to the cultural writings in the humanities.* This honor further perpetuates the role of black bibliophiles endeavoring to collect, preserve, and conserve the history of our heritage.

The intention of this paper has been to show, by a few examples, how the love and search for books can lead to incidental adventures that increase our knowledge, enrich our lives—giving them breadth and greater meaning—and satisfy our yearning to be somebody by linking us to our forebears. To me, books are not only the repositories of the past, but experiences for the present and guideposts for the future.

NOTE

* Editor's Note: The first three recipients of the prize were Dr. Chancellor Williams in 1979; Dr. Ivan Van Sertima in 1981; and Dr. Vincent Harding in 1983. Dr. John Hope Franklin was the recipient in 1986. Dr. Arnold Rampersad received the award in 1988.

Since 1985, the Phelps-Stokes Fund has managed the $50,000 endowment portfolio, and the Schomburg Center for Research in Black Culture has administered the operations for the prize.

PART V

Black-Related Memorabilia
as Collectibles and Material Culture

THE ROBESON COLLECTIONS:
WINDOWS ON BLACK HISTORY

Paul Robeson, Jr.

The extraordinary achievements and impressive mobility of Paul Robeson (April 9, 1898–January 23, 1976) have made an indelible imprint on the history of the twentieth century. His unshakable belief in the oneness of humankind has inspired people all over the world. My father's accomplishments as an athlete, scholar, singer, actor, and fighter for the freedom and dignity of all people are a dramatic reminder of the universality of the African American cultural tradition.

For the past ten years the Paul Robeson Archives, a not-for-profit tax-exempt corporation that I founded in 1973, has been assembling, preserving, and cataloging a complete record of the life and work of Paul Robeson and his wife, Eslanda Cardozo Goode Robeson (December 15, 1895–December 13, 1965). At that time, Paul Robeson gave his written consent for the archives to be incorporated under his name for the purpose of organizing and processing the more than 50,000 items in his and my mother's papers.

In 1978 I chose the Moorland-Spingarn Research Center at Howard University as the permanent repository for all of these Robeson papers, which I had inherited upon my father's death in 1976. At the same time, the board of directors of the Paul Robeson Archives agreed to deposit at the Moorland-Spingarn Research Center all of the significant number of items, including thousands of feet of film, that the archives had collected from sources worldwide and would continue to acquire.

Paul Robeson, Jr., is the son of Paul Robeson and the president of the Paul Robeson Archives. The notes and diary entries from Paul Robeson and Eslanda Goode Robeson are reprinted courtesy of Paul Robeson, Jr.

Since that time, well over 250 linear feet of documentation has been transferred from the archives headquarters in New York to the Moorland-Spingarn Research Center. Included are correspondence, unpublished manuscripts, music, legal and financial records, books, newspaper and magazine articles, phonographs and tape recordings, films, scrapbooks, ephemera, awards, and memorabilia. The documentation also includes some 20,000 photographs that record the activities of the Robeson family throughout the world.

The Eslanda Robeson papers document my mother's scholarly, cultural, and civic activities from the 1920s to the 1960s. Her collection includes correspondence, manuscripts, notebooks, photographs, and memorabilia. They are not only a rich resource for biographical study of her life, but also serve as an important source for research on her era. A woman of rare quality, Eslanda was a writer, anthropologist, lecturer, photographer, and world traveler. She also made an important contribution to Paul's early acting and singing career. Her marriage to Paul lasted forty-four years until her death in 1965. If we speak of Paul Robeson as a Renaissance man, then surely we must speak of Eslanda Robeson as a Renaissance woman. For this reason, Eslanda's papers will be cataloged separately from the Paul Robeson Collection as the Eslanda Robeson Collection.

After several years of work on these collections, the Moorland-Spingarn Research Center's opinion is that they constitute one of the largest documentary sources for historical biographical research in an American university. No comparable documentation effort has ever been undertaken. Dr. Michael R. Winston, past director of the center and Howard University vice president for academic affairs, has stated that the Paul Robeson and Eslanda Robeson Collections "mark one of the most significant milestones in the historical documentation of Black Americans."

The richness and variety of these materials can be appreciated only by examining their component categories and understanding the procedures by which the categories have been preserved and organized. Before there could be categories, there had to be a collection and for the collection special tribute must be paid to my mother, Eslanda Robeson. For it was her broad and deep sense of history and her unflagging commitment to its preservation that led her to collect and save, over a period of fifty years, the vast array of

Paul and Eslanda Goode Robeson (Robeson Collection, Prints and Photographs Department, Moorland-Spingarn Research Center, Howard University, Washington, D.C. Courtesy of Paul Robeson, Jr.)

materials that now constitute the Paul Robeson and Eslanda Robeson Collections.

WRITINGS AND CORRESPONDENCE

An article titled "Ten Greats of Black History," published in the August 1972 issue of *Ebony*, included Paul Robeson among the ten most important blacks in American history. The panel of black historians who chose him said, in part, "When his [Robeson's] scholarship is better known, he will win recognition as the finest ideologist of black nationalism since Sidney of the early 1840s. His writings will also reveal him as one of the century's most perceptive commentators on the cultures of the East, the West and Africa."

Paul Robeson, Jr.

When my mother, Eslanda, died in 1965, my father asked me and my wife, Marilyn, to take charge of the innumerable boxes of materials stored in the basement apartment of my parents' large brownstone home in upper Harlem. In one way or another, we have been working on this material ever since. For eight years, until the establishment of the Paul Robeson Archives in 1973, we spent a significant part of our free time sorting and identifying this vast mass of material. Three times we packed and moved the entire collection: first to a large apartment on Manhattan's upper West Side; then to a brownstone house in Brooklyn, where we had to move it around and protect it while the house was being renovated, and finally to the Manhattan office of the Paul Robeson Archives.

From the beginning we kept Paul's and Eslanda's papers separate, and we gave highest priority to original handwritten manuscripts and notes and to correspondence. The most important items in this category were isolated in a special subcategory.

The most significant discovery among the Paul Robeson writings was an extensive set of notes written during the period from 1932 to 1939. Originally scattered among several boxes, these notes were painstakingly assembled into what turned out to be a complete set of notes and essays on the cultures of the world viewed from an African American perspective. We eventually discovered that these writings formed virtually the entire core of Paul's articles written on cultural and political subjects during the 1930s and 1940s. Let me quote some especially vivid lines.

In some 1934 notes Paul wrote:

> Negro question confusing mainly because of American Negro who has had center of stage. He is only important insofar as he represents an African heritage and gives and receives inspiration from that source.
>
> Two ways for him [to be] American. Either in time disappear into great American mass (which Negro prefers frankly), which is a simple way—give up and disappear as race altogether. Seems to me spineless and unthinkable. [Or] to remain oppressed group—servile—also unthinkable. [Or] to become as the Jew before him—a self-respecting, solid racial unit—with its spiritual roots back in Africa whence he came. Not whining for this or that—but developing his powers to point where there is no possible denial of equality. That can never be allowed by imitating a third-rate European culture. . . .

And elsewhere in these notes he wrote what I consider to be some of the most profound lines written in this century:

The only hope for a future Negro expression among Western Negroes rests upon this pure source in Africa. . . . So the root of problem is Africa.

Africa must take the middle course.

At present [Africa] tends toward Japan's way—to become Western. . . . This comes from belief in unquestioned superiority of West and unquestioned uselessness of his own institutions. Both beliefs completely *wrong*. As background suggests, [there are] other living cultures of great importance (I select Chinese as most antithetical to Western and closest to African . . . .)

But African must know and appreciate [the fact] that . . . Western society has certainly conquered world politically and economically. . . .

Consider American Indian who has perished, and Japan who after resisting has taken it *all*—middle ground seems possible. China will probably take this. Take creations of modern science but carefully and cautiously adapt to its own culture. So borrowing from West will be mainly applied science, with culture and . . . philosophy of West rejected. (It's my belief that even an ideology as strong and fanatical as communism may later disappear into the deeper roots of Chinese philosophy. I cannot see China Western or really accepting ideology based upon Western meta-physics.)

We also discovered, piece by piece, a vast treasure trove of Paul's writings of all kinds: innumerable notes to himself concerning performances; language notes and notebooks, including hundreds of pages of Chinese calligraphy; handwritten notes for speeches and dozens of typewritten speeches with handwritten notes on them; many handwritten sheets and notebooks on music theory, as well as a completed manuscript on this topic. Among the odd scraps we found such items as his notes for a 1944 speech at an award ceremony of the American Academy of Arts and Letters, scribbled on the program for the event; notes written in English, Polish, and Russian on the concert program of a 1949 concert in a sports stadium in Warsaw, Poland; notes in English and Russian for a speech at the commemoration of the birthday of the famous Yiddish writer Sholem Aleichem in Moscow in 1959.

The most important find among Eslanda Robeson's writings consisted of detailed and vivid diaries, which she kept fairly continuously from 1924 through 1938. We found them to be not only a personal record but also a historical one. Some typical entries in her 1924 diary read as follows:

Tuesday, May 6. Opening "Emperor Jones" at the Provincetown Theatre. Paul was superb. Applause and stomping and whistling deafening after final curtain. Paul got five curtain calls. Performance really fine.

Thursday, May 15. Opening of "All God's Chillun Got Wings." Applause wonderful. All the critics were there. Standing room jammed.

Wednesday, August 27. Paul had a most interesting visit with Koriansky, the Russian critic and collaborator with the famous Stanislavsky. He is to give Paul a lesson regularly in the art of acting. Says he thinks Paul is a great artist and just needs a little technique. This is indeed a marvelous offer. They will go over "Othello" together, Koriansky suggesting and Paul learning the part. We are stunned by this good fortune.

Friday, October 17. Harry Burleigh at Ricardi's, to run over Paul's music for concert.

In her 1936 diary, that chronicled her trip to Africa, on which I accompanied her, Eslanda wrote:

June 19. . . . This was our first glimpse of inland South Africa: lonely hills and lovely valleys with cattle grazing in the spacious pastureland; table mountains one to two thousand feet above sea level; isolated farms surrounded by their miles and miles of land. And on the roads, Africans walking, Africans struggling with oxcarts . . . ; an occasional car near the towns and villages; dust. . . .

June 28. . . . Leaving Thaba N'Chu we drove out through the flat countryside, which was originally part of Basutoland but is now owned as farms by Boers. It is level fertile land, famous for potatoes. The Boers said this land was too good for the Natives and drove them back into the hills and mountains of present Basutoland . . . Soil erosion is everywhere. The rain comes down in torrents . . . and washes the soil from the slopes, making them unfit for agriculture. . . .

July 4. In the early afternoon we drove through Friedasdoorp, said to be the roughest section around Johannesburg. . . . Then we went on to the mine, called Robinson Deep. . . . There are 5,400 Natives working in Robinson Deep, and more than 2,000 additional Natives working in the next mine about a thousand yards away: Swazis, Pondos, Basutos,

127

Tuesday May 6

Opening Emperor Jones - at Provinceton Theatre. Mother, Marian and I went. Paul was superb.

applause and storm[?] and whistle deafening after final curtain. Paul got 5 curtain calls.

Performance really fine. Gilpin was there, and he and ONeill quarrelled down in dressing room after play.

ONeill and Mrs ONeill, Jas night everybody seemed thrilled with Paul's performance.

An excerpt from Eslanda Goode Robeson's diary in which she reflects upon Paul Robeson's opening in *Emperor Jones* at the Provinceton Theatre in 1924. Her account indicates that it was a magnificent performance. (Robeson Collection, Manuscripts Department, Moorland-Spingarn Research Center, Howard University, Washington, D.C. Courtesy of Paul Robeson, Jr.)

and many Portuguese East Africans.... The mine kitchens were a revelation: soup, porridge (cooked thick and shoveled out in great solid slabs onto the plates), samp [corn mush]; the meat was "cow shanks," which we found on examination to be cow feet. On workdays the men are usually given raw meat, which they cook themselves over fires built on the ground outside their rooms.

An excerpt from Eslanda Goode Robeson's diary commenting on the opening of *All God's Chillun Got Wings*, 1924. Her accounts of Paul Robeson's performances and other notes are invaluable to scholars. (Robeson Collection, Manuscripts Department, Moorland-Spingarn Research Center, Howard University, Washington, D.C. Courtesy of Paul Robeson, Jr.)

The compound is the living quarters for the Native miners only. The white workers live in their homes outside the compound, in the suburbs, or in the city. The compound is a barren dusty square surrounded by brick barracks, "rooms," and the whole enclosed by a high strong fence, very like a prison. The barracks . . . are high one-story buildings, with a door but no windows. The light and air come through ventilators placed high in the walls, just under the metal roofs. . . . I went inside one of the rooms and saw the double row of stone bunks ranged round the walls—eighteen bunks in the first tier, eighteen bunks in the second tier. . . .

The native miner has not accepted this slavery lying down. On the contrary, he has fought every step of the way. . . .

There was a great deal more of Eslanda's writings in these boxes: numerous typed speeches and lectures on a wide variety of anthropological and political topics; the original manuscripts of her three published books; the unpublished manuscripts of a number of short stories, two plays, and one novel; detailed notebooks on her trips to the Soviet Union, Africa, Spain during the Spanish Civil War, Central America, and China.

The massive correspondence in the collections covers a time span of over a half-century. Here, too, we decided to isolate the most important letters in a special category. Foremost among the thousands of letters we examined and filed were the letters between Paul and Eslanda. But we also discovered correspondence between them and a host of world figures. Imagine our excitement as we came across letters from W. E. B. Du Bois, George Bernard Shaw, Paul Laurence Dunbar, Eugene O'Neill, Rebecca West, J. Rosamund Johnson, Pandit Nehru, Langston Hughes, Theodore Dreiser, Kwame Nkrumah, Aldous Huxley, Sergei Eisenstein, Mrs. Sun Yat Sen, and Eleanor Roosevelt, to name but a few. As a whole, the correspondence provides a detailed and comprehensive view of the broad range of interests and activities pursued by Paul and Eslanda Robeson during their lifetimes. It also reveals a great deal about their personalities and about how they were viewed by others.

CLIPPINGS, EPHEMERA, AND MEMORABILIA

The clippings, emphemera, and memorabilia category in the collection seemed endless. It included newspaper and magazine articles, theater and concert programs, posters, promotion flyers, invitations and announcements, awards, gifts, and souvenirs. The clippings and programs provided a broad chronological perspective on Paul's and Eslanda's lives. They included material in many languages and covered every phase of their interests and activities. Here the task of sorting was so massive that up until 1973 we organized the material by decade and major topic only (i.e., 1930s, Theater).

In this phase of our work, we received vital assistance from Dr. Anatole Schlosser, then a Ph.D. graduate student at the New York University Drama School. In return for access to those portions of the Robeson collections that dealt with Paul's artistic career for the purpose of writing his doctoral thesis, Dr. Schlosser sorted, cataloged, and mounted a significant portion of the collection, including an important part of the correspondence. His comprehensive and meticulously researched thesis on Paul Robeson's career on the concert stage, in the theater, and in film is the seminal work on my father's artistic contributions and motivations.

PHOTOGRAPHS

Faced with what turned out to be 20,000 photographs of all sizes and kinds covering a period of about sixty years, we first divided them into three main categories: photographs including Paul, photographs including Eslanda but not Paul, photographs that included neither Paul nor Eslanda but were of people or events associated with Paul or Eslanda. Then we subdivided these categories by decade and topic, identifying the individual photographs as we went along.

Some of the breathtaking scope of this photographic collection includes the following: snapshots of Paul and Eslanda, as well as of their friends, during their college years and their years as participants in the Harlem Renaissance; photographs encompassing Paul's entire artistic career; candid photographs of Pandit Nehru and his family and of Paul and Eslanda with Nikita Kruschev and his family and friends; several thousand photographs of Paul's and Eslanda's trips to Africa, the Soviet Union, Spain during the Civil War, China, Central America, the West Indies, Western and Eastern Europe, Australia, and New Zealand; snapshots of the Robeson family and friends; photographs of Paul's political and other public appearances.

BOOKS, SOUND RECORDINGS, AND SHEET MUSIC

In the period prior to the founding of the Paul Robeson Archives, we restricted our work on books, sound recordings, and sheet music to sorting out all items of significance for future processing. For example, we assembled into separate groups all books that were written in or autographed by Paul, Eslanda, or people associated with either of them; books containing any reference to Paul or Eslanda; books used by either Paul or Eslanda as references or study aids. All phonograph recordings of Paul's voice were assembled and packed safely. All tape recordings of Paul's and Eslanda's voices were assembled and stored under appropriate conditions. Thousands of pages of sheet music were sorted according to the same basic principle: all items written on or used in any way by Paul or by his accompanist of more than thirty years, Lawrence Brown, were assembled into a separate group and stored.

THE WORK OF THE PAUL ROBESON ARCHIVES

On April 15, 1973, a Salute to Paul Robeson, a Cultural Celebration of his 75th Birthday, was presented at New York's Carnegie Hall to a standing-room-only audience. Produced by Harry Belafonte, this event provided the impetus and the funds for the establishment of the Paul Robeson Archives. The coordinator of the Salute, Ms. Roberta J. Yancy (executive director of the Twenty-First Century Foundation) became the first executive director of the Robeson Archives.

Ms. Yancy's highly professional commitment to archival procedures provided the structure for the transformation of this enormous quantity of roughly sorted materials into a well-organized and accessible collection. She set up the procedures for preserving, copying, and cataloging by year and topic all of the written and printed material, and during the next three years, work on the documents dated up to 1939 was completed under her direction. This work included the handling of innumerable crumbling newspaper articles, which were carefully unfolded and meticulously attached to a firm backing to prevent further deterioration. She also supervised all fund-raising activities and edited two archives publications—the illustrated *Biographical Journal on Paul Robeson* and a commemorative book, *Paul Robeson: Tribute and Selected Writings*—as well as directing the assembly of a large photographic exhibition covering Paul's entire career. In addition, Ms. Yancy was responsible for an extremely important achievement: two-thirds of the handwritten manuscripts were accurately deciphered and typed—some 1,600 typed pages in all.

In 1976 my wife, Marilyn Robeson, became executive director of the Paul Robeson Archives, and under her leadership the preservation, sorting, and copying of all the written and printed documentation dated through 1969 was completed. The photographs were sorted under more refined topics, and great progress was made in their detailed identification.

Marilyn also directed efforts that accomplished significant progress in new areas. All significant notes and inscriptions in books were copied, and the books were sorted into appropriate subcategories. All significant sheet music was sorted under refined topics, and some of the most important portions were copied. Three examples dramatically illustrate the importance of this work.

First, Paul had made extensive handwritten notations in dozens of books—language books, music books, poetry books, books on philosophy, chess books, volumes of plays—which revealed his thinking on these subjects.

Second, Paul's notations on a large portion of the sheet music he used revealed his musical thought and practices. From these notations it is possible to trace how Paul broke down the music of a song bar-by-bar and the lyrics syllable-by-syllable. It was through this meticulous artistic craftsmanship that he achieved such perfect diction and fluent, relaxed phrasing when he performed.

Third, a volume of Eugene O'Neill's plays carries the following inscription:

> In gratitude to Paul Robeson, in whose interpretation of Brutus Jones I have found the most complete satisfaction an author can get—that of seeing his creation born into flesh and blood; and in whose creation of Jim Harris in my *All God's Chillun Got Wings* I found not only complete fidelity to my intent under trying circumstances, but, beyond that, true understanding and racial integrity. Again with gratitude and friendship—Eugene O'Neill, 1925.

During this period significant advances were also made in fund raising. A proposal was written that resulted in a 1977 grant from the Ford Foundation, and two major benefits were successfully organized: an October 1976 Cultural Memorial to Paul Robeson's

Life, directed by Douglas Turner Ward, and a June 1978 Cultural Celebration of the 80th Anniversary of Paul Robeson's Birth, produced by Gil Noble.

The work of the archives could not have been completed without the assistance of scores of dedicated volunteers who labored patiently and diligently over the years as their contribution to the preservation of this historic collection. This was especially significant because of the very limited financial resources available to us.

My primary responsibility with regard to the work of the Paul Robeson Archives has been the development of the audiovisual collection. Over the past ten years, I have taped the several hundred phonograph recordings in the Robeson Collections and copied more than 120 hours of tape recordings consisting of Paul's unreleased studio performances, live concerts, conversations, dictations, radio broadcasts, and public speeches, as well as Eslanda's speeches.

Again, a few examples will suffice to underscore the significance of these recordings. These include an unpublished cycle of compositions by the famous Russian composer Moussorgsky; German and English versions of the aria "O Isis and Osiris" from Mozart's opera *The Magic Flute*; several highly dramatic public speeches during 1948, which was the most eventful year in Paul's life; an explanation by Paul of his concept of the Othello role in Shakespeare's play, followed by a rehearsal of one of the main monologues of *Othello* in three languages—German, Russian, and French. In addition, numerous tape recordings were acquired from outside sources.

On the basis of painstaking research and persistent effort, the Paul Robeson Archives has acquired thousands of feet of Paul Robeson documentary and feature film from all over the world. This unique film collection has been organized and developed with the able assistance of Gil Noble, producer of the WABC-TV public affairs program "Like It Is."

Finally, in April 1983 the archives presented a Tribute to Paul Robeson, a Cultural Celebration of the 85th Anniversary of His Birth, to a packed house at Carnegie Hall. Produced and directed by William Greaves, this definitive multimedia show on the life of Paul Robeson is currently being packaged for domestic and foreign educational television by William Greaves Productions in collaboration with the archives.

THE FUTURE OF THE PAUL ROBESON ARCHIVES

The principal remaining tasks of the Paul Robeson Archives are those of acquiring more Robeson materials and providing the resources for the development of audiovisual educational packages. The research performed by the archives on a global scale has located and identified many thousands of additional Paul Robeson documentary and feature films, and the Archives' board of directors has approved a plan for raising additional funds to acquire this material. The archives will also acquire some 5,000 documents from the Robeson files of the FBI, the CIA, and the State Department, which I have obtained under the Freedom of Information Act.

In addition, the vast amounts of material collected during the researching and writing of the authorized biography of Paul Robeson will be donated to the Paul Robeson Archives. This biography, published in 1988 by Alfred A. Knopf, Inc., was written by the historian, social critic, and playwright Martin B. Duberman.

Ultimately, all of these acquisitions will be added to the Paul Robeson Archives Collection at the Moorland-Spingarn Research Center.

CONCLUSION

The deposit of the Robeson Collections at the Moorland-Spingarn Research Center is a vital part of the guarantee that Paul Robeson's legacy will be available in the most complete and universal way to today's generations and especially to generations yet to come. For his legacy belongs above all to the future.

Let me end with a poem written by my son, David Robeson, with which I closed my father's eulogy at his funeral service.

> He is not mine.
> I may give him my love
> But not my thoughts.
> He passes by me,
> But he does not pass from me,
> For although he was with me in some
> ways and will stay with me in others,

He does not belong to me.
I may keep memories of him
  but not his essence,
For that will pour forth tomorrow.

MATERIALS BY AND ABOUT PAUL ROBESON

Record Albums

Encore Robeson.
  Monitor MPS-581. Selections from Paul Robeson, Jr.'s personal tape collection. Recorded 1954–57.
The Essential Paul Robeson.
  Vanguard VSD 57/58. Two-record set. Selections from other Vanguard recordings.
Paul Robeson, at Carnegie Hall.
  Vanguard VSD-2035. Selections from 1958 concert.
Robeson.
  Vanguard VSD-2015. (With chorus and orchestra) Recorded in 1958.
Robeson, Paul. *Ballad for Americans and Folk Songs.*
  Vanguard VSD-79193. Folk songs from 1958 Carnegie Hall concert.
Robeson, Paul. *Favorite Songs.*
  Monitor MPS-580. Selections from Paul Robeson, Jr.'s personal tape collection.
Paul Robeson, in Live Performance.
  Columbia Masterworks M30424. Selections from 1958 concerts at Mother A.M.E. Zion Church, New York City, and Albert Hall, London.
Robeson, Paul *Scandalize My Name.*
  The Classics Record Library, Book-of-the-Month Club, Inc., Camp Hill, PA. 17012. Three-record set.
Robeson, Paul. *Songs of My People.*
  RCA, Red Seal LM 3292. Recordings of spirituals, 1926–29.
Shakespeare's Othello. Columbia Collector's Series/Special Service Records, CSL 153. Three-record set, with Paul Robeson, Uta Hagen, Jose Ferrer, Recorded in 1946.
Showboat, by Jerome Kern and Oscar Hammerstein II. Columbia Collectors Series/Special Service Records, AC55. Paul Robeson, Edna Ferber, and Helen Morgan.
Songs of Free Men and Spirituals.
  Columbia, Odyssey 32160268. Recorded in the 1940s.

Books

Foner, Philip S. *Paul Robeson Speaks.* Secaucus, N.J.: Citadel Press. (Compilation of Paul Robeson's published speeches and writings, 1918–1974)
Editors of Freedomways Magazine. *Paul Robeson, The Great Forerunner.* New York: Dodd, Mead, 1978. (Compilation of articles about Paul Robeson and selected writings by Robeson)

Paul Robeson, Jr.

Gilliam, Dorothy Butler. *Paul Robeson, All-American.* Washington, D.C.: The New Republic Book Co., 1976.

Greenfield, Eloise. *Paul Robeson,* New York: Thomas Y. Crowell, 1975. (Biography for young children)

Hamilton, Virginia. *Paul Robeson, The Life and Times of a Free Black Man.* New York: Dell, 1974. (A biography for young adults)

Robeson, Paul. *Here I Stand.* Boston: Beacon Press, 1971. (Paul Robeson's autobiography, written in 1957)

Robeson, Susan. *The Whole World in His Hands, A Pictorial Biography of Paul Robeson,* Secaucus, N.J.: Citadel Press, 1981. (Photographs courtesy of Paul Robeson, Jr. Susan Robeson is the daughter of Marilyn and Paul Robeson, Jr.)

Seton, Marie. *Paul Robeson.* Dobson Books Ltd., 80 Kensington Church Street, London, W8, England. (Written in the 1950s and still the best biography of Paul Robeson)

Wright, Charles H. *Paul Robeson, Labor's Forgotten Champion.* Detroit: Balamp, 1975. (7430 Second Boulevard, Detroit, Michigan 48202)

Feature Films

King Solomon's Mines. Janus Films, Suite 400, 119 West 57th Street, N.Y. 10019.

Proud Valley. Janus Films.

The Emperor Jones. Janus Films.

Sanders of The River. Kit Parker Films, P. O. Box 227, Office 22, Camino De Travesia, Carmel Valley, VA 93924. Tel.: (408) 659-4131.

Songs of Freedom. Kit Parker Films.

Showboat. MGM-United Artists. 729 7th Avenue, NY 10036. Tel.: (212) 575-3000.

Documentary Films

A Profile of Paul Robeson, produced by INTERFACE for the Public Broadcasting Service. Tony Batten, Executive producer, 1975. (One-hour documentary. Available from the Public Television Library, 475 L'Enfant Plaza, S.W., Washington, D.C. 20024. Tel.: (202) 488-5000.)

Paul Robeson: The Tallest Tree in The Forest, produced by "Like It Is," WABC-TV. Gil Noble, Executive Producer, 1976. (90-minute documentary distributed by Phoenix Films, 470 Park Avenue South, N.Y. 10016. Tel.: (212) 684-5910.)

Paul Robeson:Tribute to an Artist, produced by Janus Films in cooperation with the Paul Robeson Archives. (Janus Films, Suite 400, 119 West 57th Street, N.Y. 10019. Tel.: (212) 753-7100.) [Winner, Academy Award for Best Short Documentary, 1980.]

Board of Directors of the Paul Robeson Archives

PART VI

Documenting the Black Experience:
Priorities for Collectors
and Repositories

PRESENT PROGRAMS
AND FUTURE NEEDS

Bettye Collier-Thomas

Herbert Aptheker, historian and editor of the W. E. B. Du Bois papers, in the introduction to the two-volume work *A Documentary History of the Negro in the United States*, states, "A Jim Crow society breeds and needs a Jim Crow historiography." Aptheker implies that the research and writing of history in any period reflects societal prejudices, attitudes, and practices and that a society that segregates and discriminates finds it difficult to present an objective history of a people or group it deems inferior.

Historians choose the topics they research, raise the questions they wish to see answered, and determine the interpretations that will be presented. Universities, historical societies, private and public archives, and individual collectors decide what organization and individual records should be collected and preserved for posterity. If we review and analyze the total process, beginning with the producer of the records and ending with the keeper of the records, it becomes clear that at every stage, decisions are made in light of societal definitions. Race, class, gender, ethnicity, and religion have served as beacon lights to archivists and to collectors interested in preserving the nation's history. Historically, minorities and women have not fared well in this game of choice. The achievements and contributions of Hispanics, Native Americans, African Americans, and other groups, designated for political purposes as minorities, continue to be underrepresented in works of history, in topical exhibits, and in the

Bettye Collier-Thomas is the director of the Center for African American History and Culture at Temple University.

nation's repositories. It is for these and many other reasons that this topic "Documenting the Black Experience: Priorities for Collectors and Repositories" is so important.

WHERE ARE WE TODAY?

There are three essential questions currently being addressed by historians, archivists, and collectors interested in documenting the black experience in America. The questions are:

1. What areas of black life and history have not been documented and are not now being documented?
2. What types of materials are necessary to document neglected areas of black life and history?
3. What methodology is necessary to identify and collect these materials?

The answer is that all areas of black life and history need to be documented. Some areas, or rather topics, have received more treatment than others, but, by and large, black history is still virgin territory. For the reality is that a substantial proportion of the records of black life and culture remain unidentified and in private hands. In recent years, a great deal of emphasis has been placed on documenting the people's history, an effort to focus attention less on the achievements and contributions of notables and to concentrate more on the masses, ordinary persons whose lives were undistinguished. In the field of African American history we must do both. Many major historical figures have not received attention in scholarly biographies and their papers are either uncollected or exist in fragments, scattered in a variety of general collections.

Until the late 1960s and early 1970s only a few repositories, primarily black, were actively engaged in the collection of the records of African Americans. The major repositories in which documentation of black history is a significant priority continue to be a select group of institutions, such as Howard University's Moorland-Spingarn Research Center, the Schomburg Center for Research in Black Culture, Atlanta, Fisk, Tuskegee, and Hampton universities, the Amistad Collection, and the National Archives for Black Women's History.

Even though there are records of individuals and organizations included in the collections of many other repositories, the institutions cited have the most varied and extensive collections relating to African Americans. There are also important, untapped sources of black history that lie in conventional collections, particularly those of government agencies at the local, state, and federal levels, and in public libraries and state historical societies. And there are very valuable special collections at the Library of Congress and in some university libraries. More needs to be known about the location of collected sources for the study of black history.

A brief overview of African American history suggests some of the areas in need of documentation. The history of black people in America dates back over three centuries. It begins with a few free black men who came to America as conquistadors and entrepreneurs; it moves swiftly to the importation of blacks first to serve as indentured servants and later as slaves. It is a history of struggle, a history of hope, a history of women and men engaged in a supreme effort to survive. And, while slavery was the major life experience for most African Americans who lived between 1600 and 1865, it was not the only black life experience. The country always had a free black class that continued to grow through natural increase and manumission. The earliest known black organizations were founded by free blacks.

The history of black institutions and organizations predates the Civil War. Prior to 1865, free blacks founded churches, mutual aid societies, fraternal organizations, social clubs, and literary societies. They established businesses, held conventions, published newspapers, broadsides, pamphlets, and books. In effect, the free blacks created the organizational and institutional models that provided leadership and direction for freedmen and women after 1865.

Numerous organizations and institutions were established during and after Reconstruction. New types of economic and political associations appeared that involved greater numbers of persons. Joint stock companies, banks, and a variety of cooperatives were popular. Mutual aid societies, such as the Grand United Order of the True Reformers, extended their scope of activities to include extensive real estate holdings located in a number of cities, mainly along the Eastern Seaboard. The Reformers' portfolio included banks and a variety of cooperative ventures. Independent political organizations, ward clubs, regional associations, and local and state civil rights organizations were popular in the period from 1870 to 1890.

By the 1890s black Americans were developing more sophisticated, highly structured, national organizations to carry on the many social services programs designed to elevate the masses and to develop strategies for dismantling and preventing the growth of "Jim Crow" practices and laws. It was in that period that the black woman's club movement was solidified into the first national organizations; today there are over forty-five. Between 1890 and 1920, the most important and influential national black organizations were developed. The NAACP, the fraternities and sororities, the Urban League, and numerous secular and nonsecular organizations were organized.

The major black institution in the nineteenth and early twentieth century was the church. It was a religious, social, economic, and sometimes political force within the lives of black people. The minister, as the foremost representative of the church, was assigned a very enviable status in the black community.

The advent of black normal schools (later designated as colleges and universities), black grammar and high schools, and schools for industrial education helped to create a new black elite, which was beginning to be recognized and felt by 1910. Black religious, economic, social, and educational institutions were fully developed by the beginning of the twentieth century. Between 1865 and 1900 the pool of black professionals expanded to include persons with degrees and expertise in practically every area.

What areas of black life and history have not been documented? All of the areas mentioned in this historical sketch are in serious need of scholarly attention. We will now focus in. Within each of these areas there are important materials that need to be systematically identified and collected.

SOME MISSING PIECES

I. Church records
    A. Roman Catholic Church records are usually preserved and accessible in church archives.
    B. The United Methodist Church is making a concerted effort to identify and collect the records of white and black churches. The United Methodist Church Archives at Lake Junaluska in North Carolina is in need of money and staff

for processing records received and for collecting other records.

C. African Methodist Episcopal Church records are largely scattered in church basements and belfries and in the hands of church historians who write the annual souvenir programs tracing the church's history. Thanks to historians Leon Litwack and Nell Painter, the records of Mother Bethel in Philadelphia are preserved. And thanks to historian Betty C. Thomas, the records of Bethel A. M. E. Church in Baltimore, Maryland (the second most important antebellum center of A. M. E. influence), were found and are preserved.

D. A. M. E. Zion Church records—largely scattered.

E. Colored Methodist Episcopal (now known as the Christian Methodist Episcopal Church) records—largely scattered.

F. Protestant Episcopal Church records—scattered.

G. Episcopalian records—scattered.

H. Baptist Church records—scattered.

I. Cult and sect records—unavailable.

II. Records of ministers, bishops and other church personnel— Sermons and local and regional national conference records for the most part are uncollected. The best guide to sources in this area is the reference work by Ethel L. Williams and Clifton F. Brown, *The Howard University Bibliography of African and American Religious Studies.*

III. Records of organizations

A. The records of fraternal organizations, benevolent and secret orders, literary societies, grass roots civil rights organizations, and women's organizations are largely uncollected.

1. The Grand United Order Of True Reformers
2. The Knights Templar
3. The Sons And Daughters Of Moses
4. The Gallilean Fishermen
5. The Knights Of Pythias

IV. Educational institutions—With the exception of a few black colleges, the administrative papers of most black institutions are generally scattered on the college campuses and in private hands. The records of normal and industrial schools, institutes, and training schools that went out of existence are largely uncollected. The Nannie Burroughs Collection, one example of these types of records, remained in disarray in the basement of the building that served as the National Baptist Training School for Girls. The records were discovered and given to the Library of Congress. The records of early black high schools and their graduates need to be collected.

V. Black professionals—We know so little about the growth and development of our early black professionals, who, by and large, formed the leadership at the local and state levels. There is a need to systemically identify and collect the papers of these persons as well as the professional associations they created.

high school principals	performers
teachers	scientists
college presidents	artists
lawyers	composers
physicians	architects
ministers	entrepreneurs
journalists	writers
nurses	ambassadors
editors	

VI. Newspapers, periodicals, pamphlets—The establishment of the Black Press Archives at Howard University was a major achievement. However, over three hundred of the newspapers and periodicals produced in the nineteenth and early twentieth centuries are not on microfilm and are not listed in standard directories to repositories. Researchers and collectors who discover extant issues and complete runs of these sources should contact The Moorland-Spingarn Research Center and investigate the possibility of having these records filmed. We would wish that these persons would follow the example of Professor Nell Painter, who in 1972, while working on her Ph.D. dissertation, found that the records of Mother Bethel Church in Philadelphia were kept in the church's basement where scholars using them could not adequately survey them and that they were in various stages of deterioration. She was able to bring together the church's historical committee and the Pennsylvania Historical Society so that the church's records could be microfilmed. The originals are now housed in the Pennsylvania Historical Society. The church has a microfilm reader and copy of the films and has complete control over the originals and revenue for sales of other microfilmed copies.

VII. Mass and cultural movements, local and national—We are grateful for the work of Howard Bell, Philip Foner, and George Walker in collecting and organizing data pertaining to the antebellum convention movement and the efforts of Foner and Walker to collect and edit the records of the postwar state conventions. However, there is a need to identify and collect data systematically on earlier mass and cultural movements. For example, the records of the early black expositions, exhibitions, fairs, and similar cultural efforts need to be collected. Materials pertaining to the civil rights and migration movement need to be assembled. Of course, the Martin Luther King Center for Social Change is collecting materials on the civil rights movement.

VIII. Black art and artifacts—The names of Henry Tanner, Edmonia Lewis, and several other highly visible black artists are very familiar. However, there are many other artists who were well known during their lifetime and are obscure today. We need to search out art works that they created and learn more about their lives. They frequently exhibited at the local, state, and regional expositions held during the period from 1870 to 1920.

IX. Black businesses—The records are scattered for early black banks, mutual aid associations that evolved into insurance companies, factories, and shipbuilding companies; and for that matter, so are the records of the members of Booker T. Washington's National Negro Business League.

X. Black hospitals and nursing schools

XI. Records of ordinary and undistinguished persons

XII. Women—The records of black women and their organizations, particularly national organizations, still remain largely uncollected. While a number of repositories have information on individual women and some of their local organizations, and while the National Archives for Black Women's History has a very rich collection of materials on primarily twentieth-century black women and national organizations, the majority of their records are still uncollected.

RECOMMENDATIONS

The time has arrived when bibliophiles, scholars, and researchers must cease to discuss the problem and begin to devise strategies for recovering our history through artifacts and the written word. In order to recover our history, I recommend that a permanent national committee comprised of representatives of repositories and other collecting interests be established for the purpose of setting priorities, developing strategies, and seeking funding to address problems and needs relevant to documenting the black experience. I recommend that this committee, among other things, consider the following:

1. The development of a black Union Catalog that systematically identifies materials pertaining to African Americans in repositories in America, Europe, Asia, and Africa and that includes a special section listing major private collectors.
2. The development of a national plan for undertaking local and regional records surveys that would identify organizational, institutional, and individual records that are not in a repository.
3. The development of working lists of collecting priorities, by topics, which will be updated annually. These lists will be published and made available to repositories, collectors, organizations, institutions, and others who can aid in the location of extant materials. These lists should include an identification of records created in the distant and recent past as well as current historical materials.
4. The development of a national project to microfilm endangered records that are owned by private citizens, organizations, institutions, and others who are interested in placing the materials in a repository.
5. The development of local and regional workshops that foster cooperative relationships between private collectors and representatives of repositories.
6. The development of plans to undertake documentary editing projects. Documentary histories are of great importance to the

research and writing of history. Documentary histories serve as authentic sources of our nation's history. They make available to scholars and laypersons archival materials that frequently are widely scattered in public and private repositories, archives, libraries, museums, and private collections. They can be useful sources for teachers, scholars, specialists, and nonspecialists in a variety of disciplines. Documentary editing projects are of extreme significance, since in many cases the project requires a complete survey of diverse sources and repositories. In the case of the Ratification and Black Abolitionist Projects, the Marcus Garvey and Stanton/Anthony Projects, the editors have gone out and dug up little-known materials and assembled major collections. We must do this for every topic where there is no major extant collection.

7. The development of workshops for the purpose of training community persons in oral history techniques. These workshops frequently lead to the discovery of records.

As private collectors and representatives of repositories, we all have a vested interest in the preservation of materials that document the black experience. Frequently, more emphasis has been placed on the responsibilities to be assumed by the repository. The time has come when collectors must assume equal responsibility for the rare documents and artifacts they have assembled. Collectors should make every effort to develop guides to their holdings. To protect themselves as well as their investment, they should have their holdings appraised and insured. If they choose to donate these collections to specific repositories they should determine tax options. In any case, provisions should be made for the collection to be placed in a repository or to be passed on to other responsible parties after the death of a collector. *Collectors must write wills.*

Of course, repositories have a responsibility to the donor to ensure preservation and access to collections entrusted to them.

We must find ways to cooperate. We must find ways to share. We must begin to organize so that in the year 2000 we will not find ourselves lamenting what has not been collected or preserved. It is our history. We must take care of it for posterity.

PART VII

Practical Assistance
for Private Collectors

THE ARRANGEMENT AND CARE
OF MANUSCRIPT MATERIALS

Karen L. Jefferson

The documentation of history is not, and cannot be, done by institutions alone. In fact, many of our most renowned archival institutions, like the Schomburg Center and the Moorland-Spingarn Research Center, were founded on the private collections of pioneer bibliophiles. Continuing donations from private collectors contributed significantly to the ongoing growth and development of these institutions. It is the combined efforts of the institutions and private collectors that ensure the preservation of black history for generations to come.

Once an individual or institution assumes the responsibility of collecting, the obligation to preserve these important resources accompanies that charge. As senior manuscript librarian of the Moorland-Spingarn Research Center, I, as a major part of my responsibilities, manage the arrangement and description, as well as determine the conservation, preservation, and security needs of our manuscript holdings. Private collectors are faced with a similar responsibility. No institution, no individual, can do everything in terms of arrangement and care. Choices must be made according to resources available, space, funds, and personnel. A private collector's responsibility is to learn about the range of options available, then choose what is best within his or her means.

ARRANGEMENT AND DESCRIPTION

One of the most basic premises upon which libraries and archives function is the responsibility that the user must be able to find

Karen L. Jefferson is curator of the Moorland-Spingarn Research Center.

efficiently the information within their care. To do this, librarians and archivists have developed systematic methods of what is characterized broadly as information retrieval. One of the main components in this systematic scheme is what librarians refer to as "cataloging" and what archivists call "arrangement and description." Private collectors, don't let the terminology throw you. You're doing the same thing by "putting your collection in order." The critical factor is to ensure that the "putting in order" is done in a systematic and consistent way.

In deciding upon a system of arrangement and description, consider the level of detail to which the collection will be processed. This will depend on your resources and access needs. The level of arrangement and description denotes the units or amounts of materials to be handled; i.e., a box, a folder, or individual items. In the Manuscript Department of the Moorland-Spingarn Research Center we generally arrange and describe to the folder level. However, because of overwhelming research requests, we arrange and describe correspondence and photographs to the individual item level. The level of arrangement and description to which you process should meet two basic needs: control and security—knowing what's in the collection and being able to find efficiently the materials needed.

Arrangement

Generally, a manuscript collection is arranged by subject and/or by form. Within this scheme materials may be arranged numerically, alphabetically, chronologically, or by a combination of the three. Choose an arrangement scheme that is best for you, and stay as consistent as possible with it. Keep it simple; the fewer exceptions the better.

In choosing your scheme, consider these two questions: (1) What is the most logical access point? (2) What is the scope of your resources to maintain the arrangement system? If you most often need to locate the materials by the subject, an alphabetical rather than a chronological filing system may be the most efficient. As you know, materials cannot be arranged to meet every access point. As does the library, you may need to develop different finding aids to meet the varying points of access. In the library, books are arranged on the shelf in one consistent systematic scheme. However, the card catalog allows for manipulation of each individual item by a number of access points: author, title, subject.

What is the scope of your resources to maintain the arrangement system—the time and workforce required to add new materials, to refile materials, and to produce the varying finding aids for the access desired? Again, keep the arrangement system simple. An elaborate system that you cannot maintain is like having no system at all.

In deciding upon a system of arrangement, there are two guiding principles archivists use: "provenance" and "original order." These two principles are concerned with maintaining the integrity of the collection. Provenance requires that materials from different collections *not* be intermingled. For example, Moorland-Spingarn Research Center has letters of Dr. W. E. B. Du Bois in numerous collections. However, we would not combine these letters to create an artificial collection on Du Bois. To do this would detract from the original collections and take the Du Bois letters out of the context in which they were created.

Original order requires that materials remain in the arrangement in which the creator maintained them. This principle primarily refers to organizational records. However, it has application to personal papers as well. There is some flexibility in adhering to the principle of original order, for oftentimes personal papers have no discernible arrangement scheme, or the arrangement may be too cumbersome for practical use. The caution here is to review the collection before you arrange the materials. Determine if there is in fact an arrangement scheme already in place and whether that scheme is a practical one. Sometimes you may not have to rearrange the collection at all. Or you may simply make minor adjustments to make the arrangement consistent.

There is one sure way to test how efficient and logical your arrangement system is. Can you or others find what is needed with ease?

Description

Description focuses on two general areas: finding aids and descriptive labels. Finding aids are the key to the various access points to locate materials in the collection. You must determine what finding aids you need and can maintain within your available resources. In the Manuscript Department we keep a number of finding aids: collection files, registers, and location, donor, subject, and name indices. Each of these aids provides a wealth of information for a variety of access needs. Producing and maintaining these aids requires a good deal of staff time, especially when they are produced manually.

Descriptive labels are also important, not only as tools for access, but to help to document the significance of the materials you collect. I cannot stress strongly enough that you take the time to label your materials thoroughly and accurately. You may label by units, i.e., a box or folder of materials, or by the individual items: photographs, for example. Without proper labeling some of the materials you collect will be virtually lost to history. An undated letter written to "Dear Sir" and signed with the first name only may have less significance if the researcher cannot identify the correspondents. Or a photograph of a group of people may have little significance unless one realizes it is a photograph, say, of the participants in the founding meeting of the Niagara Movement.

Labeling is important and should be done as soon as possible. Your memory may lapse and the details you initially recalled so clearly may fade with time. Labeling can help retain this invaluable information.

To reiterate, take the time to establish and maintain a system of arrangement and description. Keep it as simple and as consistent as possible. The time you invest now in this sometimes tedious task will save you invaluable time when you need to find materials in your collection. Also, this is an investment for security, for you will know what is in your collection. This information will help you in assessing your collection for insurance or financial purposes and in considerations for future acquisitions. Access to your materials is critical.

CONSERVATION

Conservation is the preventative care of materials to help deter the deterioration process. Conservation is the single most important action you can take in the physical care of your collection. As the saying goes, "An ounce of prevention is worth a pound of cure." From a financial perspective, conservation becomes a very practical choice. Repairs and restoration once materials have been damaged are very costly, oftentimes prohibitive, and in some cases the materials may be damaged beyond repair.

Deterioration of materials usually is the result of two basic factors: the environment in which the materials are kept and the inherent properties of the materials. In conservation, a primary concern is to control the environment in which the materials are kept.

First consider where the collection is housed. Unfortunately, many irreplaceable objects are too often housed in areas that are potential sources for disaster—the attic, the basement, the spare room that just happens to be below the bathroom or kitchen. Institutions often have similar storage problems, where space is at a premium, and there are literally no alternatives for housing the collection. Your responsibility is to be conscious of the potential dangers and to take preventative measures to protect your collection from harm. Inspect the area carefully inside and out for water pipes, heating and cooling units, electrical wiring, drainage systems. Consider the possible problems that can occur, and take steps to minimize the danger.

In addition, these four tips are helpful as preventative measures:

1. Don't store materials directly on the floor. Storing materials even a few inches off the floor can save your collection from water leaks and spills that, I have concluded, are inevitable.
2. Don't store materials directly against the wall. The walls may be conductors for heat, if a source of heat (radiators, oven, computer) is located near the wall. Also water leaks from ceilings and roofs may travel along the wall.
3. Don't stack materials carelessly to precarious heights. Not only can the materials be damaged from haphazard storage, you may be hurt in trying to retrieve them.
4. Finally, refrain from eating, drinking, and smoking around your collection. Food may attract unwanted pests that will feed upon your collection along with your crumbs. Getting rid of insects can be very expensive; you may have to fumigate your entire collection. With liquids, accidents do happen, and liquid spilled on a document can stain or literally remove the writing from the page. The fumes from smoking are harmful pollutants to your collection. On this, little more need be said than the old adage, "Where there's smoke, there's fire."

To help protect your collection you should maintain a temperature between seventy to seventy-five degrees fahrenheit and a relative humidity of 50 to 60 percent. Central air conditioning is one way to maintain this atmosphere control. Central air conditioning also serves as a ventilation and filtration system for circulating and cleaning the air of harmful pollutants such as aerosols and gases, dust, and dirt. However, central air conditioning may not be a feasible solution for you. The key point to remember is to at least keep the temperature and humidity at a constant level. Fans, heaters, humidifiers, dehumidifiers, and air filters may help resolve this crucial problem.

Just as important as temperature and humidity is the control of light, artificial and day light. Items exposed to unfiltered light may fade, discolor, and weaken the structure of the material. To resolve this problem, ultraviolet filters for light fixtures are widely available and relatively inexpensive. In addition, closed boxes and containers help prevent damage to materials from dust, dirt, and light.

The kind of boxes and containers materials are stored in is an important conservation measure. It is generally accepted by archivists that it is best to store materials in acid-free containers that buffer the materials from acid migration. In that way, the acidic qualities in a box, folder, or other items cannot easily migrate among the collection. Acid-free containers are relatively expensive compared to regular containers, but they are an investment well worth your consideration.

As stated previously, deterioration usually results from environmental factors, but it can also be caused by the inherent properties of which the materials are made. So concern must be placed in arresting the deterioration factors, and even further, restoring materials already damaged.

Conservation is an ongoing, rapidly changing science, where better techniques are continually being sought and developed. A general rule of thumb is reversibility. Consider carefully before applying any preservation measure that cannot be *undone*.

There are a number of professional conservators who do restoration and repairs, and you may contact them for advice. However, use of conservators may be a relatively expensive proposition. There are some preservation measures you can do yourself.

1. Unfold materials and store them flat. Each fold in an item is a

stress point, which over time will become the area where the item will break.

2. Remove metal fasteners from materials. Most metal fasteners will oxidize and rust. Plastiklips, stainless steel clips, and staples are alternative fasteners. Although relatively more expensive, they are a practical investment considering how rusting metal fasteners will eat through a document. Remember all fasteners are stress points on materials. When possible, avoid fasteners and store the attached materials together in a folder so the individual items won't be separated and lost.

3. Avoid use of tape or glue to mount or mend documents. The adhesives in most tapes and glues are harmful. In many cases, over time, the adhesive will dry out and the item will become unattached. The adhesive may leave an unremovable stain.

4. Mending documents that are torn is a relatively simple process. There are special tissue papers and paste that can be used, and the repair will be barely visible. This process can be mastered with practice. Depending on the value of the document and the extent of damage, mending may require a professional conservator.

5. Sometimes the best course of action is to make a copy of the item. The copy will be for use and the original item will be retired for all but exceptional cases. Copies in the form of a photocopy, a photograph, or microfilm should meet most needs.

6. Encapsulation, a process of sandwiching a document between two clear mylar sheets, is a very easy process to master. The sheets are sealed with a special double-sided tape. Encapsulation allows handling and viewing of fragile items. Encapsulation can hold fragments of an item in place without glue or tape, and it is reversible. However, encapsulation increases the amount of space needed to store an item since the thickness has increased threefold. Note: materials should be deacidified before encapsulation or the item will continue to deteriorate.

7. Deacidification is the process of removing the acid qualities in a document and depositing a buffer to guard against further acid buildup and deterioration. In considering deacidification, the document must be tested for the suitability of the paper and ink. Deacidification is a process of which you should be aware, although you may not want to try it yourself. It is a protective measure you may want to have done by a conservator.

8. Although usually thought of in terms of exhibiting, mounting and framing can be preservation measures. You've already been cautioned against use of glue and tape. To mount materials it is better to hold the items with pressure, using mylar corners and strips. Another caution here: if you must make scrapbooks, invest in sturdy paper, preferably acid-free. Generally, paper for scrapbooks is of poor quality and quickly becomes brittle and fragile. One additional point on scrapbooks: refrain from including pressed flowers, which may serve as food for pests. In framing, be sure to adhere to archival standards, use acid-free materials, and seal the frame to protect against dust and dirt. Ideally, documents should be cleaned and deacidified before framing.

CONCLUSION

This presentation is a broad overview of arrangement and care of your collection. But there is much more of which you should be aware. To help you to increase your knowledge in this area I suggest the following:

1. Become familiar with archival and conservation literature. There are numerous organizations including the Society of American Archivists, the American Association for State and Local History, the American Library Association, and the American Institute for Conservation. Each of these organizations publishes materials that are extremely helpful.
2. Attend conferences and participate in workshops offered on arrangement and conservation. These workshops are primarily organized for archivists and librarians, but they are generally open to anyone.
3. Finally, visit and tour archival institutions, libraries, and conservation centers. Talk with the professionals there. Most will be more than happy to discuss their work and give helpful suggestions on arrangement and care.

RESOURCES

Organizations to contact for further readings, conferences, and workshops:

Society of American Archivists
600 South Federal Street
Suite 504
Chicago, IL 60605

American Association for State and
  Local History
1400 Eighth Avenue, South
Nashville, TN 37203

American Library Association
50 East Huron Street
Chicago, IL 60611

American Institute for Conservation
Klingle Mansion
3545 Williamsburg Lane
Washington, DC 20008

THE ARRANGEMENT AND CARE
OF SMALL BOOK COLLECTIONS

Valerie Sandoval Mwalilino

The true bibliophile possesses a collection of some sort and may want to organize, appraise, sell, or preserve that collection. I offer suggestions for accomplishing these tasks, and they are just that: suggestions, not commands. I come by my knowledge largely through my experience as head of the Acquisitions Section at the Schomburg Center for Research in Black Culture, a position I have held since 1977. Not only have I examined, evaluated, and recommended nearly every one of the 2,000 items we add per year, but I also take acquisition trips, and meet collectors, dealers, and donors of all kinds. Part of my job is to recommend conservation measures such as microfilming and binding. I also possess an insatiable curiosity about the world of books and printing, especially as it relates to black people.

ORGANIZING

Mrs. Jean Blackwell Hutson tells a story about when she was a library student and working part time at the 135th Street branch library. Eager to apply the principles of the Dewey Decimal System to Mr. Schomburg's private collection, which was newly acquired by the New York Public Library, she stayed late one night and arranged all of the volumes by Dewey. When Mr. Schomburg came in the next day

Valerie Sandoval Mwalilino is now the coordinator of the African/Middle Eastern Acquisitions Section at the Library of Congress.

and saw what she had done, he was furious! He could not find any of his books because his own organization system was by size and color of volume, not subject (which is the basis of Dewey). As a result, he banished her from the library "forever."

I relate this story in order to illustrate my main point, that organization is not really all that important as long as you can find what you need. This pertains to the private collector, even though some small libraries have an informal attitude toward cataloging certain parts of their stacks.

However, if you feel overwhelmed by the disarray, or you possess so many books that it taxes your memory to recall what you've placed where, then there are a few things you can do. First, how do you remember a book? Does the author's name come first to your mind or does the title? Or do you remember "that red book with the gold lettering?" Work with whatever way is easiest for you.

If you only remember authors, then arrange your books alphabetically by author's last name. Maybe it's the librarian in me, but my own collection is shelved by subject—history, biography, fiction, etc. You can even file by size, color, chronologically by date of publication, or whatever. Any system that works for you is fine. Now there are some bibliophiles who may wish to go beyond these simple measures. This will be to your advantage in other areas, such as appraisal and insurance. For you, I recommend giving work to all these unemployed or marginally employed librarians out there by contracting them to catalog your books completely. I know of one librarian in San Francisco who is able to support herself with free-lance cataloging of private collections. One collector recently hired a student to compile a bibliography of his books on blacks in the military. It was quite an impressive list when the student finished, and she told me that he had plans to computerize the file.

Cataloging involves making up a bibliographic record of some kind, including place of publication, name of publisher, year published, number of pages, and edition. Other information can be added, such as birth and death dates of author, size of book, volume number, etc. For those who like to keep meticulous records, I suggest you note when the book was purchased and how much you paid for it. This information helps immensely if you plan to insure or appraise the collection.

APPRAISING

A professional appraisal consists of having an expert examine your collection and produce a signed, written statement describing the contents of your library and assigning a dollar value assessed at "fair market value."

Bear in mind that the appraiser is a professional who charges a fee for his or her services. The fee structure depends on the extent of the collection in question and the amount of time required to do a thorough evaluation. If a collection is small or not particularly valuable, the appraiser may charge a flat fee or waive it entirely. The terms are negotiable.

There are several reasons why an appraisal should be done. The most common reason is for tax purposes. If you decide to donate your collection to a university or a nonprofit institution, the appraisal is proper evidence when claiming a tax deduction. If you decide to assign your own value to the donation, beware of inflating it to unrealistic proportions, especially if you are audited by the Internal Revenue Service.

The same principles apply if you want to insure your collection against fire or theft. Insurance is a definite consideration if you have a very valuable collection of rarities or even only a few rare items. If you've already insured your house and other possessions, it makes sense to include your book collection, too. However, insurance is an expensive proposition these days, so talk to your agent about the cost. The knowledgeable appraiser can advise you on all these questions, but you may need to consult legal and tax specialists as well.

The appraiser is an expert on books, but it is not so easy to find an expert on black books. We are all too aware of the fact that black materials have traditionally been undervalued in terms of historical and commercial importance. Early black collectors often acquired their books at a very cheap price because dealers did not feel that black material was worth much. Today there is more appreciation for black literature, due to a number of historical factors, not the least of which is the black consciousness movement of the sixties and seventies.

The best way to locate an appraiser is to contact the Antiquarian

Booksellers Association of America (see Resources at the end of this chapter). They can provide you with an ABAA national membership directory. This directory will include an index to the booksellers' subject specialties, such as black studies, art, Americana, women. Many of the booksellers are also appraisers.

If you don't wish to employ an appraiser, you can try the do-it-yourself method. This exercise will not substitute for a professional appraisal, but at least it will give you some ballpark figures to play with when assessing the monetary value of your collection. Before you begin, it is wise to familiarize yourself with the basic terminology used in the book trade.

The first step is to sort out and organize your volumes either by subject or alphabetically by author's last name; note on cards all the pertinent bibliographic data mentioned previously. A short description of each book should follow, indicating whether it has hard or soft covers, illustrations, plates, fold-out maps, a dust jacket, etc. In addition, briefly describe the condition of each book (e.g., good, clean, missing back cover) and any other relevant information, such as "autographed by author."

Next, consult the latest annual volume of *American Book Prices Current* and *Bookman's Price Index*. These sources will indicate what a comparable copy of your book sold for in a recent sale. If a copy has not been sold lately, you may have to consult earlier volumes. *American Book Prices Current* lists only those books that sold for at least twenty dollars at auction. *The Bookman's Price Index* listings are based on a description of books offered for sale by leading dealers.

A professional appraiser, being familiar with recent sale prices, adjusts these figures, allowing for any circumstances or peculiarities of the book in hand. There are no hard-and-fast rules for this calculation, but certain factors, such as age, condition, and scarcity weigh heavily. For example, in 1979, a first edition novel by Paul Laurence Dunbar entitled *The Uncalled* (New York, 1898) sold for forty-five dollars. It had the original decorated cloth covers characteristic of his books and was in fine condition. Suppose there was one just like it in your collection that was inherited from a family member. Suppose also that since this relative was a friend of Dunbar, he autographed her copy with an endearing salutation. In addition, Dunbar enclosed a letter that was pasted into the inside cover of the book. The value of your copy would then be substantially higher than that 1979 sale price.

If you've done all this homework and still wish to hire an appraiser, all of the perviously cited information that you've compiled is still useful. These facts will help to get a more accurate and fair value assessment, especially if the appraiser has no expertise in black-related materials.

SELLING

If you are planning to sell your books, mention this to the bookdealer. If a dealer buys the collection, you may not get top dollar, but dealers usually pay in cash. Many novices are not prepared for the disappointment of low prices because they make the mistake of assuming that some musty old tome found in their basement will bring them instant wealth. Be advised that bookdealers are in business to make money and they are really offering you the equivalent of a wholesale price. They hope to sell it to another collector, at a customary markup of 100 percent.

If you prefer to sell your books at auction, you must contact an auction house, many of which are listed in *American Book Prices Current.* Selling by this method may fetch higher prices, but it is a very slow and time-consuming process, assuming that the auction house is interested in handling your lot. You may not even realize payment for at least six months, depending upon the auction house's schedule. Nonetheless, it is worth investigating if you have a valuable collection.

A third alternative is to sell directly to another collector, avoiding a middle person. This can be done by advertising your wares in a local newspaper or in a national literary magazine that takes ads. The *AB Bookman's Weekly* is a specialist publication that is widely read by people in the book trade. An ad in this journal will reach a large audience of collectors and dealers alike. If you are personally acquainted with many collectors, you may want to hold a house sale the way people sell their furniture in "tag sales." Whichever method you choose, the thing to remember is to keep your overhead low and your prices reasonable.

PRESERVING

I am not a trained conservator, but I can recommend some routine measures you can follow in order to preserve your valuable collections. The following is a list of *do's* and *don'ts*.

First, whatever you do, do not use transparent tape to mend tears or for anything else. This tape was meant only for temporary use. It does considerable harm to paper over time by yellowing, cracking, and leaving a residue on the pages. The same applies to the use of rubber bands. Do not use them to tie papers or documents together. Use cotton twine instead.

Second, do not make any permanent markings in the books using ballpoint pen, ink, or marking pens of any kind. If you must note anything, use pencil and mark lightly. Do not affix any glued labels on spines or covers. A small, unobtrusive "ex libris" bookplate on the inside cover is all right for ownership documentation.

Third, do not insert miscellaneous papers between the pages of books, especially items on newsprint. If you really need to keep a newsclipping of an important item relating to the author together with your book, make a photocopy of the piece on bond paper and discard the original clipping. Or else, enclose the clipping in a mylar (an interplastic) sleeve before putting it inside the book. Do not keep bookmarks in between the pages for a long time unless you know for a fact that the bookmark is made of acid-free paper. Cheap quality paper such as newsprint has a high acid content and it will discolor paper adjacent to it when the acid "migrates."

A word on handling: please do not crack open the spine on new books or force open old covers. This destroys the bindings and weakens the spine, which in turn makes the pages fall out. Do not shelve books with the fore edge down and the spine up because it warps the covers and bends the pages. This may sound elementary, but please do not use a book as a coaster for wet glasses. I have seen too many volumes with water rings staining the cloth and leather outer covers. Also, do not use books to prop open windows or as doorstops. Use a brick if you must keep the door from slamming shut. Extremes of temperatures should be avoided to preserve the life of your books. So, if your bookshelves are in front of the radiator or under the air conditioner, please consider moving them. The same holds true for extremes of humidity and dryness. Try not to store your books in the basement where it is damp because they can become moldy.

When you buy a new book, prolong the life of the dust jacket by removing it while you read the book and replace it when finished. When marking the place where you stopped reading, don't turn down the corners of pages or fold the pages in half. Also, do not use metal paper clips to mark pages because they will rust eventually and leave stains on the paper.

If you have some softcover items that need rebinding in hard covers, please stop to reconsider. Many bibliophiles feel that rebinding enhances a book. Sometimes it does, but I have seen too many examples of eighteenth-century books in nineteenth-century bindings. This in itself is not a crime, but the binder usually cuts the margins down to such an extent that the value of the original suffers. Trimming margins may also affect part of the text. I say leave the pre-nineteenth century books alone. Have a professional binder make a box for it, really a simple task. The appendix to this paper indicates how to contact binders and suppliers of conservation materials if you wish to follow up on my suggestions.

A final word on conservation: with proper handling and storage, your books will last longer, retaining and even increasing their value as artifacts of culture.

STARTING YOUR OWN COLLECTION

Don't despair if you do not have a collection yet; it's never too late to start building one. Even if you do have some accumulation of books in your home, it's not really a collection as such unless it was acquired with a purpose. Look over your present titles with an eye for quality and consistency.

Quality refers not only to the intellectual content of a book, but its physical properties, too. This means that you may not wish to keep all those cheap supermarket paperbacks, old college textbooks, most dictionaries, encyclopedia sets, some Book-of-the-Month Club selections, and scattered issues of recent popular magazines and newspapers. *Do* keep novels, poetry books, literary magazines, and monographs by prominent authors, especially first editions.

Consistency can be determined when a collecting subject or theme is adhered to. A good collection reveals something about the owner's major interests and thoroughness, and it should be near to complete in one or several subject areas.

Beginners should try to confine themselves at first to one field or subject at a time, such as poetry or music. Early black collectors often attempted to document the total black experience in print, an ambitious goal, even in the nineteenth century. Today, one would require at least a ten-story building to house such a collection. Just to put things in perspective, the Schomburg Center spends over $100,000 every year acquiring books on black culture and we are by no means completely exhaustive in our holdings, even though we probably have 90 percent of what's available.

In whatever field you are collecting, know how to identify the various editions and printings of the literature. Bibliographies are indispensable guides to this information and they can provide a standard against which you can measure the completeness of your efforts. Extremely useful is Monroe N. Work's *Bibliography of the Negro in Africa and America*, often cited in dealer catalogs. There are many excellent bibliographies available on all phases of black history and culture. You might ask a librarian in your area to recommend some.

Once you've chosen a subject, what type of book should you look for? I prefer hardcover books to paperbacks because they tend to last longer. I know collectors who acquire paperbacks anyway for trading purposes. Detective and science fiction as well as comic books and novels are hot items. When you buy a hardcover book, don't throw away the jacket. If it's a secondhand book you're choosing, look for one that's clean and in good shape.

A book does not have to be old to be worth something. Works by modern and contemporary authors, especially first editions, are easily accessible and are a wise investment for the future. These works can usually be bought for a relatively cheap price, but they tend to increase in value over the years because they are creative efforts that go out of print quickly. Some well-known examples are the novels of Langston Hughes, Claude McKay, Zora Neale Hurston, and any writer of the Harlem Renaissance period.

First editions are usually more valuable than later ones, but fully revised or variant editions should not be overlooked. If the author is living, say for example, Toni Morrison, try to get her or him to autograph your copy.

Acquiring older titles and rare books is a bit more complicated and generally expensive. If you are well versed in the field, then you won't be so likely to spend a lot of money on a forgery or a fake. Specialized antiquarian bookdealers and auction houses tend to have high-priced books, but reputable places will usually vouch for the authenticity of goods offered for sale.

Now that you know what you're looking for, where do you find the books you want? The obvious answer is, of course, the bookstore, but there are many kinds of bookstores around. You have the first-run type such as B. Dalton, which features books hot off the press. These are good places to browse for new first editions. B. Dalton's New York City store regularly hosts authors who are in town to promote their books, so that's a great way to get an autograph. The only person I've stood in line for is Sidney Poitier when his autobiography, *This Life*, came out. It was certainly worth the wait because all the women got a kiss along with their autograph.

The other kind of bookstore is one that sells books that are no longer in print. Most dealers have some sort of specialty such as art books, but there are some good general secondhand collections like the Strand in New York where you can almost always find something about everything. The ABAA directory will give you some idea of the diversity of these kinds of booksellers. Many do a mail-order trade and will accept orders for items not currently in stock. Collectors who become regular patrons sometimes can expect special treatment. For example, the dealer may be aware of the fact that you are dying to get a Phillis Wheatley for your collection, but none have come on the market. Even though others may have made the same request, he may give you the first opportunity to bid on it, if you are a preferred client.

Where else besides bookstores does one search for books? Keep an eye out for local library rummage sales. People often donate their unwanted books to the library, and there you may find some gems. The library may withdraw books from the shelves or sell off duplicates. However, these books are usually marked with property stamps and glued pockets for circulation cards, which lessen the value slightly. Flea markets are similar sources of cheap goods, even though you may find more in the way of collectible memorabilia than printed matter.

Another, mostly overlooked, source of books is your own family.

Do you have any older relatives with their own collections? School teachers, especially, are known to acquire interesting reading matter. Has anyone recently inherited personal effects from a deceased family member? Ask permission to search their belongings for books; you may come up with some good nineteenth-century titles.

The same sources to which you would go for books are also excellent for locating old and antique photographs. If you come across these, by all means pick them up and hold on to them. Collecting nineteenth-century photographs is a growing field. Black photographers are poorly if at all documented in the literature and history of the industry. The photograph as cultural artifact is a burgeoning field of scholarly research activity in general and practically unexplored territory as far as the African American experience is concerned.

CONCLUSION

The definitive textbook on black book collecting has not yet been written. Information can be located here and about, but for those who seek to learn more, the best source is collectors themselves.

Black bibliophiles and collectors have a deep interest in acquiring and preserving a priceless heritage. There is something about the printed word that is enduring in a way that other forms of recordings are not. This is not to limit our scope, but print orientation is a way of life that should be carried on, not rendered obsolete by new technologies.

It doesn't matter if your book collection is huge or of modest proportions; we all should be concerned about documenting the black experience in whatever capacity. And who knows, over time and with the right conditions, you may have a library named after *you* one day.

RESOURCES

I. To locate book dealers:

Antiquarian Booksellers Association of America
50 Rockefeller Plaza
New York, NY 10020

II. Related reading matter:

AB Bookman's Weekly
P.O. Box AB, Clifton, NJ 21230

III. To find book services:

LMP; Literary Market Place; Directory of American Book Publishing
(New York, R. R. Bowker) (lists various book related services including
custom bindery)

IV. Conservation supplies and information:

TALAS
104 Fifth Ave.
New York, NY 10011

Hollinger Corporation
3810 So. Four Mile Run Drive
Arlington, VA. 22206

Assistant Director of
    Preservation
Administrative Dept.
Library of Congress
Washington, DC 20540

American Association of State and
    Local History
1400 Eight Ave. South
Nashville, TN 37203

National Conservation Advisory
    Council
S.I.356
Smithsonian Institution
Washington, DC 20560

Northeast Documentation Conser-
    vation Center
Abbot Hall
24 School St.
Andover, MA. 01810

PART VIII

Summary and Closing Remarks

SUMMARY

James Turner

Being involved in examining the work and significance of black bibliophiles and their collecting activities has a certain personal dimension beyound the average intellectual appeal. Reclaiming our black past has become increasingly important to me especially in light of situations I face daily. Recently, I sat in a meeting with administrators at the institution at which I work. They decided that they would recognize what they would call Presidential Scholars, and as a result the president was going to ask each of these young people to say who was the most important teacher in their experience. The university was going to go into the community and honor this Presidential Scholar and the teacher. Imagine that kind of publicity at a time when the baby boom is almost over, and the competition for new recruits at the university is important. But nonetheless, in the content of that meeting, I suggested that perhaps they also might include other people besides the high school teachers, such as people in the community, the churches, street academies. Of course, the administrators said no because they didn't see how ministers or church groups were significant. I tell that story only to say that when we talk about black bibliophiles, particularly their history in Harlem and in New York from 1940 roughly up to 1960, we're talking about teachers who had a very great effect upon the youth in their community and upon the community at large.

J. A. Rogers, Richard B. Moore, and Lewis Michaux cannot be ignored if the complete social and intellectual history of our folk in urban America, particularly Harlem, during the period 1940 to 1960 is to be fully told.

James Turner is the founder-director of the Africana Studies and Research Center, Cornell University.

The role of black bibliophiles and collectors in our intellectual and social history has been an honorable tradition. Their contribution has been varied and complex through the annals of our history. But, on the whole they have gone unrecognized and consequently unhonored. This collection of papers is a much needed exchange of ideas and information about black bibliophiles and collectors. Such an exchange goes a long way in correcting this rather inexcusable oversight in our community.

Black bibliophiles for the most part have been self-initiated and self-motivated. Their collections were largely self-financed. Their commitment to the collection of books about African people and their descendants in the world was usually a life's obsession. They were like any people with interest in books, who respect the search for truth and the pursuit of new vistas in knowledge. But they were perhaps distinguished by their rather specific task and special mission. And as such they were pioneers in the field of African history and African American studies long before many people appreciated the importance of what we now call black studies.

Whether Arthur Schomburg, Carter Woodson, or Daniel Murray, they were for the most part marginal persons, at times ignored by their colleagues in academia, shut off from financial support for their research, and most critically shut away from intellectual discourse and the exchange of ideas and sources. But still they persisted with the strength of their determined will and the motivation of the mission they had taken upon themselves: the necessary responsibility to defend the name of black folk against the prevailing theories of biogenetic determinism, which we commonly refer to as racism. These bibliophiles and collectors were concerned about what Robert Hill referred to in his paper, "On Collectors, Their Contributions to the Documentation of the Black Past," as the ease with which our people's history has been lost. Their task was not only to refute the racist ideologies that shamefully passed for scholarship in so many American schools and publications, but they were intent on retrieving the vital sources of history and providing the groundwork upon which future generations could build.

The black bibliophiles and collectors provided for us a basis upon which to build. In this sense they were visionaries. They kept the faith of the race with confidence that one day we would turn with interest and appreciation to these materials. For this we owe these forerunners our interminable respect. They stood as beacons of hope and inspiration when others were disinterested or despairing.

What is noteworthy about the black bibliophiles is that not only did they collect books, they also wrote books. They therefore interpreted the prevailing sources from what we now refer to as an Afrocentric perspective—all that simply means is they didn't look from the outside in, they looked from the inside out. They took black folk as the focus, and as such they provided for us an alternative to eurocentrism.

Subsequently, they were mentors. They collected and wrote books, but also, they spoke. They spoke to the people regularly. They understood implicitly Carter Woodson's rejoiner against an education that separates the educated from the masses. They had difficulty understanding the rationale for a scholarship that did not, as Mari Evans has proclaimed in her poem, "Speak the Truth to the People." For them that was the primal task. The black bibliophiles had a definite concept of the role of scholarship, and as such they were forceful mentors. They were confident of the propriety of what they were doing. They believed profoundly in education and they encouraged it at every opportunity. But they believed in education for a purpose—to rescue, to defend, and to contest issues of distortion as Tony Martin referred to in his paper, "Bibliophiles, Activists, and Race Men."

They also believed very profoundly, when it was largely in doubt, in the educability of black people. They did not reduce the level of discussion when they went from one place to the next. When I saw J. A. Rogers down at the Student Center at New York University in 1959, his level of discussion about his books *Sex and Race* and *Nature Knows No Color Line* was a basic theoretical refutation of biogenetic determinism at the same level as when I heard him in discussions at Lewis Michaux's place on 125th Street, at Richard B. Moore's forum over the Stetson hat shop next to the Apollo Theatre, or often in John Clarke's basement library. It was Richard B. Moore who put in my hand Gerald Massey's *Egypt Light of the World* at a time when I was nineteen years old and in a street gang. He gave me Count Volney's *Ruins of Empire*, which I use today in teaching; it is hard to get now.

Lewis Michaux, an unknown but significant person in the renaissance of Harlem, owned, on the corner of 125th Street, the largest bookstore in Harlem. It was one of the few places in the black community where one could purchase *Presence Africane*. That illustrates, I believe, the point that Tony Martin made earlier about the pioneer bibliophiles' global view as well as their sense of the study of the black world community and their Pan-African contacts among intellectuals.

EXTENDING THE MISSION

I would like to encourage the study of black, grass roots institutions and activists. This is perhaps the most difficult subject for scholars because there is a kind of intellectual chauvinism that permeates the academic world that says that grass roots people are marginal—what they have done is without portfolio whether it offers something to us or not. Most white academics are often freer than black academics are. They could take an Eric Hoffer off the dock front, without any degrees (this happened while I was a student), and offer him a visiting lectureship at the University of California. We suffer from a syndrome that makes it difficult for us to see the significance of grass roots studies, but I want to suggest today that we do just that.

Robert Hill discussed in his paper the difficulty of studying black radicalism, and I agree. There is a clear bias in the prevailing African American historiography, and black radicalism is not treated. That some African American historians would teach their students about the civil rights movement with no reference to Malcolm X, with no reference to the Nation of Islam, is an illustration of what might be ideology but is not pedagogy, that is, not honest pedagogy. No one can tell the story of that period and all of its consequences in the humanities, in social and political thought, without examining Malcolm X.

In closing, I am particularly pleased that Howard University took the lead on this exchange. Preserving our history is a serious matter. Our black collections are endangered. I'm concerned whether our black collections will have a share of the new technology in our institutions so that those collections can be preserved. This is a very important issue in a period when we see a shift in national political direction that might mean support for new technology. This shift might challenge us to be much more concerned about planning for the preservation of our institutions from our own resources, falling back on that which the black bibliophiles always had to rely on, community support.

Last, I don't think we can afford to wait another fifty years to suddenly recognize the importance of the Garvey Papers, especially when we know the tendency to ignore and to distort our peoples' contribution to American and world history is still very active and forceful. So it seems to me what contemporary bibliophiles do can greatly affect the visibility and strength of that contribution. Our work continues.

CLOSING REMARKS

Michael R. Winston

When I was invited to make final remarks, I was asked by Dr. Elinor Sinnette to give "a concluding sermon." Those were her exact words. I said that after so many papers, no one would be interested in a sermon. At best, I would attempt a "brief benediction."

There are few things that I am more proud of than the "Black Bibliophiles and Collectors" symposium, the papers from which make up this volume. Dr. Sinnette, Mr. Paul Coates, and Dr. Thomas Battle developed the black bibliophiles and collectors project. It was clearly overdue. They had the vision and the imagination to first conceptualize it and then acquire the necessary resources. A great debt is owed to them for organizing the conference and for editing this volume.

In this benediction, I want to highlight the thinking of the men who founded the American Negro Academy, which we know through the excellent study *American Negro Academy: Voice of the Talented Tenth*, by Professor Alfred J. Moss, Jr. They wanted to provide an institutional means to make available the collections of many of the members as a solid basis for serious scholarship. Two members, Kelly Miller and Jesse Moorland, worked particularly hard to bring Howard University into association with the academy. It is not by accident that the Moorland Foundation, as it was called, was established at Howard University in 1914.

Those acquainted with black people's history, as well as the history of individual collectors and organizations, know that one of the tragedies of black history is the great efforts made in isolation— heroic individuals who worked against odds that are now difficult to imagine, but who were often defeated simply by the circumstance of their isolation. Far too many of the bibliophiles and collectors discussed

Michael Winston is vice president for academic affairs and former director of the Moorland-Spingarn Research Center.

at the symposium *could have* made even greater contributions had they not had to labor under crushing burdens. The symposium and this volume are first steps in reinforcing the network that has always existed in a rather tenuous way among collectors, scholars, and what Mr. Coates calls "lay-historians"—a term that I have adopted and think is extremely useful.

Professor James Turner, in his summary, suggested that J. A. Rogers, and others like him, have been disregarded. I no longer think that those men are really on the periphery; I think that we are beginning to understand them in a different way. I think that black American scholarship is, in fact, achieving some new peaks of maturity on all of these matters.

But black Americans are in danger of not institutionalizing very much of that maturity. Though I am concerned about our institutional life and the challenges we face, I am also very encouraged by the response that black bibliophiles, scholars, and researchers have made to this call. When the conveners and I first discussed this project, there was some question in our minds whether there would really be enough of a response to justify university sponsorship and to give us the hope that this would be a continuing program. I am pleased that the response to the symposium and the anticipation of this volume have been such that obviously we must find the means to continue this kind of activity. We must find the means of anchoring such endeavors institutionally in a way that these will continue long after those of us who are concerned with it today have passed from the scene. We have at least seen the beginning of some very important interactions surrounding the issue.

Some of the collectors who attended the symposium have said to me, "At last, a university is prepared to take us seriously and provide the kind of technical assistance that has been so difficult to get." Collaboration between collectors and higher education institutions is essential. We at Howard need to make it a vital and important part of our university and facilitate such collaboration at other institutions.

This volume is an interactive tool. It is our desire that the information given in this volume will crystalize areas of black history and will motivate bibliophiles, collectors, and research repositories to communicate and to seek out information so that culturally and historically valuable materials will be unearthed and preserved.

APPENDIX A

Gallery of Bibliophiles

WILLIAM HENRY DORSEY

October 23, 1837–d.?

William Henry Dorsey was a prominent nineteenth-century bibliophile, collector, and artist. One of the earliest of the Philadelphian collectors, he was the son of Thomas Dorsey. The elder Dorsey escaped from slavery in 1836 and settled in Philadelphia, where he became one of that city's most distinguished and successful caterers. Upon his father's death, William received an inheritance which enabled him to pursue a largely successful career as an artist. His collecting efforts, which began when he was a youth, continued throughout his life. He became widely known for the large assemblage of books, memorabilia, and other items collected during his lifetime. This collection was displayed in Dorsey's "museum," and was one of the earliest efforts to document the accomplishments of black Americans by placing them in a museum setting. (Photo courtesy Dorsey Collection, Manuscripts Department, Moorland-Spingarn Research Center, Howard University, Washington, D.C.)

DANIEL ALEXANDER PAYNE MURRAY

March 3, 1852–December 31, 1925

Daniel Murray was born in Baltimore, Maryland, and received a basic education from schools in Baltimore and Washington, D.C. In 1871 he was appointed personal assistant to Ainsworth R. Spofford, Librarian of Congress. He remained at the Library of Congress for fifty-two years. In 1900 he compiled a preliminary list of 270 books by "Negro" authors. By 1904 the list was expanded to five thousand books. Murray worked for twenty-seven years on a mammoth project—a six volume "Encyclopedia of the Colored Race," which was never published. Murray was largely responsible for establishing a Negro collection at the Library of Congress and by provision of his will his personal library of over fourteen hundred books was added to that collection. (Photo courtesy Murray Papers, Manuscripts Department, Moorland-Spingarn Research Center, Howard University, Washington, D.C.)

KELLY MILLER

July 18, 1863–December 29, 1939

Kelly Miller was the leading proponent for the establishment of a separate Afro-American research collection at Howard University. He was a professor of mathematics and sociology, 1890–1934, and dean of the College of Arts and Sciences, 1907–1919. Dean Miller succeeded in persuading the Reverend Jesse E. Moorland (1863–1940), an alumnus and trustee who was a secretary of the YMCA, that he should donate to Howard his sizeable private library on black people in Africa and in America, so that the university might develop a "Negro-Americana Museum of Library" that could be a center for research and instruction. (Photo courtesy Miller Papers, Manuscripts Department, Moorland-Spingarn Research Center, Howard University, Washington, D.C.)

JESSE E. MOORLAND

September 10, 1863–April 30, 1940

Jesse E. Moorland was born in Coldwater, Ohio. In 1891 he graduated from Howard University's Theological Department. He was ordained and did missionary work in North Carolina and Virginia. In 1907 Moorland was voted a member of Howard University's Board of Trustees.

Dr. Moorland developed an extensive collection of books and other items bearing on the history of people of African descent. It was acquired by Howard University in December 1914 as a gift from Dr. Moorland. At the time, his collection was considered by many experts "probably the largest and most complete yet gathered by a single individual." (Photo courtesy Moorland Papers, Manuscripts Department, Moorland-Spingarn Research Center, Howard University, Washington, D.C.)

HENRY PROCTOR SLAUGHTER

September 17, 1871–March 14, 1958

Henry P. Slaughter received a degree from Howard University's School of Law in 1900. Slaughter, a printer and newspaper publisher, decided after graduation not to practice law, but chose instead to continue his career as a printer, working for the Government Printing Office.

Slaughter began collecting books as a young man and actively collected throughout his life. At one time his library numbered more than 10,000 volumes. In addition to books, Slaughter maintained a file of 100,000 newspaper clippings and 3,000 pamphlets on the history of race relations and slavery. The Slaughter collection is now housed at the Atlanta University Center, Robert W. Woodruff Library. (Photo courtesy Slaughter Papers, Atlanta University Center, Robert W. Woodruff Library, Division of Special Collections and Archives, Atlanta, Georgia)

ARTHUR ALFONSO SCHOMBURG

January 24, 1874–June 10, 1938

Born in Puerto Rico of a black mother and German father, **Arthur Schomburg** emigrated to New York City in 1891. The search for his own identity led him to become a foremost lay historian, lecturer, and collector of books and other materials to document the history of people of African descent. Arthur Schomburg's collection was broad in scope and contained thousands of books, manuscripts, pamphlets, paintings, and selected realia dealing with the black experience in Africa, Europe, the Carribbean, North, South, and Central America. In 1926, the Carnegie Foundation purchased Schomburg's collection and deposited it in a Harlem Branch of the New York Public Library. From this nucleus, the Schomburg Center for Research in Black Culture was begun. (Photo courtesy Locke Papers, Manuscripts Department, Moorland-Spingarn Research Center, Howard University, Washington, D.C.)

ALAIN LEROY LOCKE

September 13, 1885–June 9, 1954

Alain Locke, philosopher, educator, and critic of the arts, was born in Philadelphia, Pennsylvania, and attended schools in that city. He received a B.A. degree from the Philadelphia School of Pedagogy in 1904. He completed the four-year course at Harvard in three years, was elected to Phi Beta Kappa, and was the first and only African American selected for a Rhodes Scholarship during his lifetime. Locke was appointed to the faculty of Howard University in 1912, where he was instrumental in promoting the study and teaching of black history. In 1925, Locke edited an issue of the *Survey Graphic* that was devoted to the "New Negro" as reflected in the art and literature of the period known as the Harlem Renaissance. This was later published in book form as *The New Negro*, a seminal work of the period. Locke became an intermediary between patrons of the arts and black writers and artists of the period, becoming somewhat of a "godfather" to the "New Negro Movement." Locke was a staunch supporter of cultural pluralism and one of the most significant and influential intellectuals in the first half of the twentieth century. Locke was an avid collector of African art and books related to people of African descent. Upon his death, his various collections were willed to Howard University. (Photo courtesy Locke Papers, Manuscripts Department, Moorland-Spingarn Research Center, Howard University, Washington, D.C.)

RICHARD B. MOORE
August 9, 1893–August 16, 1978

For many years **Richard B. Moore** was a well-known Harlem book dealer, collector, historian, and lecturer on subjects dealing with Afro-American history. Moore was born in Barbados in 1893 and brought to the United States by his stepmother in 1908. He began his career selling books from door to door. In 1942 he opened a book shop on 125th Street in Harlem. Moore acquired thousands of books dealing with black subjects and used his collection as a means of refuting stereotyped misrepresentations of black people and their history. His collection is now housed at the University of the West Indies, Barbados. (Reprinted from *Flamingo* magazine, London, England: Chalton Publishing Company, n.d. available)

GLEN CARRINGTON

May 7, 1904–June 12, 1974

Glen Carrington was a Howard University graduate, class of 1925. He was an active student leader and editor-in-chief of the *Bison*. Carrington began collecting books while still a student and continued to collect over a period of fifty years. In 1975 after his death, his collection of more than 2,200 books in fifteen languages, 500 recordings and other memorabilia, most pertaining to the Harlem Renaissance, was acquired by the Moorland-Spingarn Research Center. (Photo courtesy Carrington Papers, Manuscripts Department, Moorland-Spingarn Research Center, Howard University, Washington, D.C.)

APPENDIX B

Biographies of Contributors

Charles L. Blockson, a native of Norristown, Pennsylvania, was educated at Pennsylvania State University, where he excelled as an athlete. His collecting activities began at an early age, and today his library of books, pamphlets, and documents relating to the black experience numbers over 80,000 items. In 1984, his collection was deposited at Temple University, where Mr. Blockson has been appointed its curator. A member of several state and national literary and historical societies, he lectures on black culture at schools, universities, and historical associations throughout the nation. Mr. Blockson's published works include *Pennsylvania's Black History*, *Black Genealogy*, and *The Underground Railroad in Pennsylvania*. Mr. Blockson has received an honorary doctorate from Villanova University in Pennsylvania.

Minnie Harris Clayton earned her master's degree in library science from Atlanta University School of Library and Information Studies. She was trained and certified in archival administration at the Georgia State Archives. Formerly librarian-archivist of the Martin Luther King, Jr., Center for Social Change, she is presently the director of the Division of Special Collections and Archives, Atlanta University Center, Robert W. Woodruff Library. Her writings include "Martin Luther King, Jr., A Selected Bibliography"; "A Survey of Archival Holdings Related to the Black Experience in the Civil Rights Movement"; and *A Guide to the Southern Regional Council Archives, 1944–1966.*

Bettye Collier-Thomas is director, Center for African American History and Culture, Temple University. A graduate of Atlanta University, she earned the doctor's degree in history from George Washington University. A diligent researcher, she has held faculty and administrative positions at several colleges and universities, including the University of Maryland, the College of William and Mary, and Howard University. Dr. Thomas has written and spoken extensively on the subject of neglected sources in the study of African American and women's history. In 1979 she served as one of the principal organizers of "The First National Scholarly Research Conference on Black Women," and in 1980 she organized "A National Conference on Black Museums."

Betty M. Culpepper is assistant chief librarian for Technical Services and Automation, Moorland-Spingarn Research Center. She is a graduate of Howard University, Kent State University, and Catholic University. She has earned master's degrees in library science, history, and public administration. Ms. Culpepper formerly served as chief, Washingtoniana Division, District of Columbia Public Library. She is an active member of the Afro-American Historical and Genealogical Society.

Robert A. Hill is associate professor of history at the University of California at Los Angeles, where, since 1977, he has also served as editor-in-chief of the multi-volume *Marcus Garvey and Universal Negro Improvement Association Papers* (University of California Press, vols. 1–7). He is also the compiler of Marcus Garvey's *The Black Man Magazine* (1933–39) and Cyril Briggs's *The Crusader: Official Organ of the African Blood Brotherhood* (1918–1922). He is presently completing work on his compilation of *The Rastafari Bible*. Mr. Hill was born in Kingston, Jamaica, and received the M.Sc. degree from the University of the West Indies.

Clarence Holte's interest in black American history began at Lincoln University in Pennsylvania where he was challenged by African classmates (among them Nigeria's Nnamdi Azikiwe) to answer queries about Afro-American history. He began to read and acquire books on the topic, and over the years his private collection grew to approximately 8,000 volumes. The collection was purchased by the Nigerian government in 1976 and is now housed at the Kashim Ibrahim Library of Ahmadu Bello University in Zaria, Nigeria. Mr. Holte has written numerous articles and essays, under a pseudonym, for *National Scene*, a literary supplement to many of the nation's black newspapers. In addition, he is the author and editor of *The Nubian Baby Book* published in 1972. In 1982, Lincoln University awarded him an honorary Doctor of Laws degree.

Jean Blackwell Hutson attended the University of Michigan, Barnard College, and the New School for Social Research and studied for three years with the late Professor Leo Hansberry, an authority in the field of African antiquities. Mrs. Hutson received her master of library science degree from Columbia University in 1936. She was awarded the honorary degree, Doctor of Humane Letters, from King Memorial College, Columbia, South Carolina. During a career spanning four decades, Mrs. Hutson has served in a variety of positions. From 1949 until 1980 she was curator, then chief of the Schomburg Center for Research in Black Culture in New York City. Among Mrs. Hutson's publications are numerous bibliographies, the preface of *Dictionary Catalogue of the Schomburg Collection of Negro Literature and History*, and "The Schomburg Collection," in *Freedomways*, a quarterly review, 1963. Mrs. Hutson retired from the New York Public Library, September 1984.

Karen L. Jefferson was appointed curator of the Moorland-Spingarn Research Center in 1987, having previously held the position of senior manuscript librarian (1980–1987). She is responsible for the overall program development and supervision of the Manuscript Division, including directing acquisitions, arrangement and description, and concerns for the conservation, preservation, and security needs of the collection. Ms. Jefferson is a graduate of Howard University and Atlanta University, where she received the master of library science degree. She is a certified archivist and has gained additional training by attending numerous workshops, seminars, and classes on basic and advanced archival administration, and the preservation and conservation of archival materials. Active in archival professional associations, she is a strong advocate of community participation in the preservation of historical materials.

Tony Martin is professor and chairman of black studies at Wellesley College, Massachusetts. He received his M.A. and Ph.D. in history from Michigan State University and the B.Sc. in economics from the University of Hull, England. In 1965 he qualified as a barrister-at-law at Gray's Inn, London. He has taught at the University of Michigan-Flint, the Cipriani Labour College (Trinidad), and St. Mary's College (Trinidad). He has been visiting professor at the University of Minnesota, Brandeis University, and The Colorado College. He has written and edited several books, including *Literary Garveyism: Garvey, Black Arts and the Harlem Renaissance; The Pan African Connection; Marcus Garvey, Hero;* and *Race First: The Ideological and Organizational Struggles of Marcus Garvey and the Universal Negro Improvement Association.*

Valerie Sandoval Mwalilino obtained her master's degree from Columbia University's School of Library Service. In 1988, she joined the Library of Congress as coordinator of the African/Middle Eastern Acquisition Section (AMEAS). From 1977 to 1988, Mrs. Mwalilino was head of the Acquisition Section and technical service coordinator at the Schomburg Center for Research in Black Culture, a major research division of The New York Public Library. Together with the center's archivists, she developed guidelines to identify and protect rare black books. Her writing has appeared in various publications, including *The Schomburg Center Journal, Black Enterprise, Nuestro,* etc.

Paul Robeson, Jr., the only child of Paul and Eslanda Robeson, worked closely with his father during the turbulent period from 1948 to 1959 and was a participant in many of the events which shaped his father's destiny. He is president of the Paul Robeson Archives, Inc., and has spent more than a decade assembling and cataloging a vast collection documenting his father's life and work. He has written extensively on the life and legacy of Paul Robeson. Mr. Robeson has also served as principal consultant for documentary films about his father, including the Oscar-winning "Paul Robeson: Tribute to an Artist" by Janus Films. Mr. Robeson is a graduate of Cornell University and presently resides in Brooklyn, N.Y.

Elinor Des Verney Sinnette investigated the role of black bibliophiles and collectors while conducting research for her doctoral dissertation. Her book, *Arthur Alfonso Schomburg, Black Bibliophile and Collector, A Biography,* was published by Wayne State University Press in 1989. Educated at Hunter College, Pratt Institute, and Columbia University's School of Library Service, Dr. Sinnette has been active in the library profession for over forty years. She has held positions in The New York Public Library, The New York City Board of Education, and has served as an educator and consultant in Nigeria and Kenya. Her articles have appeared in several professional journals. She contributed "The Brownies Book: A Pioneer Publication for Children" to *Black Titan: W. E. B. Du Bois, An Anthology,* published by the Beacon Press. Since 1987, Dr. Sinnette has been chief librarian of the Moorland-Spingarn Research Center.

Jessie Carney Smith has been university librarian and professor at Fisk University since 1965. She was educated at North Carolina A & T State University, Cornell University, Michigan State University, George Peabody College of Vanderbilt University, and the University of Illinois, where she received the Ph.D. degree in library science. Dr. Smith has directed workshops and internship programs for librarians and served as consultant to library and research programs in the humanities. She has lectured widely on developing black collections, collecting black memorabilia, and black and ethnic genealogy. Dr. Smith has contributed numerous book reviews, articles, and special reports to professional journals and other publications. She is the author of *Black Academic Libraries and Research Collections: An Historical Survey* and is editor of *Ethnic Genealogy, Images of Blacks in American Culture*, and *Notable Black American Women*.

James Turner is the founder/director of the Africana Studies and Research Center, Cornell University. He graduated with honors from Central Michigan University and earned the M.A. in sociology and certificate of specialization in African Studies from Northwestern University, and the Ph.D. in political sociology from the Graduate School of the Union Institute. Since 1961, encouraged by Richard B. Moore, he has been a collector of books and materials of eighteenth- and nineteenth-century origin dealing with Africa and Americans of African descent. Dr. Turner has contributed to the *Cornell Review*, the *Western Journal of Black Studies*, *Black Books Bulletin*, and *The Journal of Negro Education*. His article, "Sociology and Black Nationalism," appears in Joyce Ladner's *Death of White Sociology* and is considered a significant contribution to the subject. His recent book, *Theoretical and Methodological Issues in Africana Studies*, has received wide acclaim in the field.

Dorothy B. Porter Wesley, curator emerita of the Moorland-Spingarn Research Center, began her work as curator of the Moorland Foundation in 1930. Under her leadership the Foundation, and later the Moorland-Spingarn Collection, became a major repository for the study of black history and culture. During a career at Howard University that spanned forty-three years, Mrs. Porter Wesley attracted numerous donors, developed the library and manuscript collections, and, most importantly, assisted researchers from all over the world. Mrs. Porter Wesley is a graduate of Howard University, and in 1932 received a master's degree in library science from Columbia University. Her publications are numerous and include: *Early Negro Writing 1760–1837; Negro Protest Pamphlets; North American Negro Poets*; and *Afro-Braziliana, a Working Bibliography*. She is also a contributor to the recently published *Dictionary of American Negro Biography*. In 1971, as a tribute to her accomplishments, the University of Susquehanna bestowed the Doctor of Letters degree upon Mrs. Porter Welsey. She was honored by Syracuse University in 1989 with an honorary Doctor of Humane Letters.

INDEX